TRADE AND SUPPLY CHAIN FINANCE

PURE AND SIMPLE

FUNDAMENTALS, TOOLS, AND PRACTICE GUIDE

Stephen Atallah

TABLE OF CONTENTS

Overview

This book provides a comprehensive and practical guide to understanding and using contemporary Trade and Supply Chain Finance (TF), using plain, jargon-free language, to make TF better understood and more accessible to finance professionals, business managers, students, lawyers, regulators, or anyone starting or considering a career in the field. TF refers to a group of financial products, solutions, and structures by which a bank or other any other type of Financier provides or risks its funds to provide Buyers time to pay for their goods or services, or to ensure that their Sellers get paid on time. All forms of TF achieve at least one of these two prime objectives, while often delivering additional benefits to its users. This material explains TF's most widely used tools and risk-mitigating techniques, and their shared fundamentals that underscore all TF products and solutions.

This book's initial chapters explain TF's fundamentals, key terms, players, and core principles that form the foundation of all TF solutions. Chapter 1 provides a strategy that any user can use to analyze any TF opportunity or challenge in order to structure an optimal TF solution. In Chapter 2, key TF risks are identified, followed an explanation of the leading TF risk mitigation tools and techniques in Chapter 3. The subsequent chapters explain the various types of TF products and solutions used the most throughout the world and how TF is funded and documented. The final two chapters focus on emerging FinTech and industry trends, and the broad range of career opportunities existing today throughout the industry.

TF is one of the oldest forms of finance used throughout the world, having evolved over time to encompass a wide range of highly specialized products adapted to each user's needs, abilities, risk tolerance, and local market conditions. As a result, one of the biggest challenges to understanding or learning about TF now is that it is mostly understood and delivered as a random assortment of independent and unconnected specialties, often provided by single-solution specialists. For example, for any given financing objective, there are often several different ways to mitigate risks and document, fund, and arrange a transaction, each of which can produce significantly different outcomes for the parties. A specialist in medium-term export finance, for example, is not likely to know how, or to be tasked, to arrange short-term import finance, or to know whether it is more advantageous to use Trade Credit Insurance instead of a Letter of Credit (LC) or an Export Credit Guarantee to manage risk for a particular transaction. To identify the most appropriate products and solutions, the full range of possible and appropriate TF resources and solutions would need to be considered. This book's purpose, therefore, is to present a holistic understanding of TF as a coherent universe of financial solutions that share common fundamentals to achieve their prime objectives.

Every business in the world finances itself in one way or another to meet its TF, working capital, or other financing needs. Many businesses rely on some form of TF in the form of short-term credit (e.g., 30-day Credit Terms) provided by its Sellers. Others, however, may finance themselves by simply relying on their cash flow from sales or by taking out loans secured against their assets (e.g., inventory, accounts receivables, real estate, personal guarantees, etc.). TF is but one financing option a business can use to meet its needs, and in many cases, TF can provide a more cost-effective solution compared to other types of finance. The better TF is understood, the more it can be used to benefit business of any size.

In the past, the term TF referred only to cross-border imports and exports, with financing solutions focused heavily on mitigating cross-border risks. In reality, however, the vast majority of TF is used to support domestic trade among businesses buying and selling goods or services within their own country. Thinking of TF as being limited to only international trade explains in large part why TF is learned and discussed primarily as a niche international banking product rather than a more universal domestic corporate finance solution. The term TF, as used throughout this book, therefore, more accurately covers TF as both a domestic and international financing solution.

Another common misconception is the exaggerated role banks play in TF. The vast majority of TF is provided not by banks or other finance companies, but by businesses that sell goods or services. The most common example of this occurs when a Seller gives its Buyer a set number of days, usually 30, to pay for its goods or services. Banks and other finance parties are involved in much less (probably less than 20%) of all TF done domestically or globally. Another obstacle to understanding TF is the numerous and often redundant product labels it goes by. For example, Receivables Purchase Finance, Invoice Discounting, and Factoring all refer to the same TF solution. Similarly, Supply Chain Finance, Vendor Finance, Confirmed Payables, and Reverse Factoring all refer to the same TF solution. Depending on the location and type of user involved, there may be slight variations in each solution's application.

ABOUT THE AUTHOR

The author has over 30 years of real-world TF transaction experience as a global and domestic trade and supply chain finance banker, trade credit insurance underwriter, and international trade attorney. He has structured and executed the leading forms of TF covered in this book in the most challenging credit markets and business environments. His career started as an attorney for the United States' national Export Credit Agency—the US Export-Import Bank (EXIM)—negotiating international trade deals with business and governments throughout the world, using loans, guarantees, letters of credit, trade credit, and political risk insurance. He went on to lead TF businesses for global banks before heading the North American underwriting group for the world's second largest trade credit insurer and advising emerging blockchain companies and other FinTechs. He is an internationally recognized trade and supply chain finance expert and speaker at industry forums and events, as well as a contributor to industry publications.

CHAPTER 1

TF Fundamentals, Key Terms and Mechanics

Understanding TF fundamentals and the key terms used in its structuring and execution is essential to learning how to use, market, and execute TF products and solutions successfully. The key industry terms explained below and used consistently throughout this book have been selected and defined carefully and precisely according to their actual meaning. These terms are used and understood globally throughout the TF industry, though some practitioners may use alternative terms and names based on local customs and practice.[1] These terms apply to TF transactions for the purposes of this book, even though many of them may apply equally to other non-TF financial transactions. For example, the definitions below include a TF "Seller" (a business that sells goods or services), which is not the same as other non-TF Sellers (e.g., businesses that sell real property). The use of key terms will often be qualified with "generally" or "typically" to point out when there may be exceptions to how things are "generally" done in the real TF world. For example, generally a Buyer will pay a trade Financier's interest and fees, but not always—sometimes a Seller will pay all or a portion of them to make its sales terms more competitive. Generally, a Seller will extend short-term credit to its customers, but not always—some Sellers may extend longer terms or none at all. It is important throughout this material to understand and appreciate when exceptions and flexibility may occur so they may be used when structuring or innovating TF solutions.

STRUCTURING TF

A TF *structure* or *solution* is a financial arrangement designed to achieve the transaction parties' objectives. TF providers also often use the term "*solution*" as a marketing term to indicate that some superior level of transaction customizing is being used to satisfy client needs. A TF *product* is a predesigned *structure* or *solution* that is *offered for sale* by a Financier or other TF provider (e.g., banks, guarantors, Trade Credit (TC) Insurers, etc.).

---

1   To emphasize that these terms are standard in the industry, they are capitalized throughout the text.

A transaction's structure, whether simple or complex, will define how its risks and rewards are allocated among each party based on their obligations stated in their transaction agreements and by applicable laws. Transaction structuring is often focused on mitigating transaction risks, but it is also used to achieve non-risk-related objectives, such as lowering transaction costs, increasing profitability, or making the transaction risks and rewards easier to sell, share, and transfer to other parties.

Universal TF Structuring Formula

The formula for structuring an optimal TF transaction, complex or simple, in which each party achieves its objectives as much as possible should always involve the arranging parties performing the following analysis, in the following order, to identify the following.

1) Each transaction party, its role, and its objectives (e.g., Seller, Buyer, Financier, Guarantors, Service Providers).

2) Possible products or solutions to achieve those objectives (Loans, Open Accounts Credit Terms, Letters of Credit).

3) Risks to using each possible product or solution. (Buyer payment default, Seller contract breach, Financier or Guarantor insolvency, Political Risks).

4) Risk mitigation tools available for each risk. (Payment default insurance, third-party guarantees, trade credit insurance).

5) Costs of implementing each product or solution. (Fee, interest, funding costs).

6) Optimal solution that achieves each parties' objectives as closely as possible.

Highly skilled TF arrangers follow this process, consciously or not. But any TF party, not just bankers or other experts, can structure an optimal TF solution by following this process as long as they understand and apply TF basics and possess the skill to know how and when to partner with experts (lawyers, Brokers, credit specialists).

TRANSACTION PARTIES & OBJECTIVES

Sellers

Sellers are businesses that sell (transfer legal title and possession of) their goods or services (Items) to a Buyer in exchange for funds.

A Seller's TF objectives may include:

a) being paid on time, whether before, at, or after it delivers its Items to its Buyers.

b) increasing its sales by offering existing and potential Buyers time to pay in the form of competitive Credit Terms.

c) minimizing its risk of Buyer nonpayment and related financing costs.

d) accelerating its cashflow from sales to reduce the number of days sales are outstanding and unpaid ("DSO" in accounting terms) in order to help it leverage and optimize its working capital to sustain or grow its business.

Exporters

Exporters are Sellers of Items to a Buyer in a country other than the Seller's country.

Buyers

Buyers are businesses that buy (take legal title and possession of) Items in exchange for delivering funds to its Seller. Most businesses, at some stage in their business cycles, will be both Sellers and Buyers, depending on whether they are buying materials to transform into Items to sell or are selling finished Items.

A Buyer's TF objectives may include:

a) having as much time as possible to pay for its Items in order to optimize its working capital management to grow its business. The more time a Buyer is given to pay, the more time it has to use and leverage its cash on hand to operate its business and to reduce its need to borrow working capital funds from other creditors. In many cases, a Buyer's ideal Credit Period would match the time at which the Buyer is paid by its Buyers. In many cases, Buyers would not be able to afford Items without being allowed to pay over time. This is especially true for purchases of expensive capital equipment that takes time to generate a sufficient return on the investment into it. Accordingly, a big factor in a Buyer's selection of its Sellers is whether they provide sufficient Credit Terms at a competitive price. A Buyer may also want the ability to pay its Seller early in exchange for receiving an "early pay" discount, when that discount exceeds its normal cost of capital. In summary, a Buyer will use TF to:

b) pay the lowest possible financing costs;

c) afford Items it would otherwise not be able to purchase without Credit Terms;

d) take advantage of any "early payment" discounts offered by a Seller, when the Seller's discount exceeds the Buyer's normal cost of capital;

e) select Sellers based on the type of Credit Terms they or their Financiers can offer.

Importers

Importers are Buyers of Items from a Seller in a country other than the Buyer's country.

Obligors

An Obligor is the party obligated to pay any form of TF-related debt to a Financier. Obligors can include Buyers, Borrowers, or other debtors.

Financiers

Financiers are businesses that provide, or put at risk, funds to enable a Buyer to pay for its Items over a period of time or to ensure that the Seller is paid on time. Financiers may be Sellers that allow their Buyers time to pay, or banks, non-bank finance companies, governments, or any other business type that provides TF. It is important to remember that Sellers, not banks or other finance companies, are by far the largest providers of TF globally and domestically, by allowing their Buyers a period time to pay for their Items, typically within 30 or more days from delivery. Governments or international agencies may also act as Financiers to support TF transactions in order to promote specific public interests, which often involve some form of trade promotion, such as national export or foreign policy promotion (e.g., Export Credit Agencies) or promoting economic or social development in countries in need (e.g., World Bank Agencies).

A Financier's TF objectives may include:

a) earning a rate of return on the funds it puts at risk that is sufficiently in excess of its cost of capital and consistent with its payment default risk and other risks it takes;

b) maintaining maximum flexibility to cancel or modify the term of its TF transactions if in its opinion, its risks, transaction costs, or rates of return change;

c) for some publicly owned Financiers, promoting public policy objectives, such as export or foreign policy promotion, as discussed further below in the Chapter 3 section on Agency Finance.

Lenders

Lenders are Financiers that provide TF in the form of *loans* to Obligors that are also referred to as "Borrowers."

Guarantors

Guarantors agree to pay an Obligor's debt to its Financier in the event the Obligor fails to pay it.

Trade Credit Insurers

Trade Credit Insurers are private or publicly owned businesses that insure Financiers against the risk of nonpayment of their trade-related debt caused by their Obligor's financial inability to pay.

Political Risk Insurers

Political Risk Insurers are private or publicly owned businesses that insure Financiers or other TF transaction parties against the risk of nonpayment of their trade-related debt or other financial losses caused by Political Risks.

TF Service Providers

TF Service Providers are businesses that provide various types of services to facilitate TF, including Trade Credit Insurance Brokers, FinTech Platforms, lawyers, banks, governments, and international agencies.

KEY TERMS

Trade

The "Trade" in TF occurs when a Seller delivers Items to a Buyer in accordance with their legally binding purchase and sales agreement, or their sales contract, which may be written or otherwise evidenced by the parties actions, in which one party's offer to buy or sell Items is followed by the Seller's delivery of the Items. The Trade, in this context, is often referred to as a "sale" in common business speak, but not in this book because the meaning of a Trade encompasses more elements that a mere "sale." The term "sale" can, for example, also refer to the value of pre- or post-delivery Items that are later disputed, returned, or discounted, whereas Trade represents the value of delivered Items that are not returned and for which there is no dispute in terms of quality, quantity, or legal obligation of the Buyer to pay.[2]

A Trade is usually initiated with a Buyer placing a purchase order, transmitted electronically or verbally, to buy Items from a Seller. In such cases, the Buyer's purchase order would constitute its offer to buy the Items, which is then accepted by the Seller as evidenced by the Seller communicating its acceptance of the offer or by the Seller simply delivering the requested Items in accordance with that purchase order. In many cases, a Buyer and Seller may be engaged in a series of Trades over time, and for the sake of efficiency, they may decide to enter into a written master sales agreement that contains specific terms and conditions (prices, quality, etc.) that will apply to each of their future Trades. Their sales agreement would, for example, state how purchase orders may be communicated, how and when the Items are to be delivered, and a description of any warranties or other conditions that may apply to each Trade.

Trade Accounts Receivable (AR)

A Trade Accounts Receivable is a Seller's legal claim for payment against its Buyer for Items delivered in accordance with their Trade agreement and for which the Seller has extended the Buyer a specific period of time (e.g., 30, 60, or 90 days) after delivery to pay for the Items. For example, when a Seller delivers Items to a Buyer on March 1 and agrees to allow the Buyer to pay for them on April 1, the Seller has created a legal claim for payment against that Buyer, called a "Trade Accounts Receivable," "Receivable," or "AR." This form of short-term Seller financing directly to its Buyer is the most widely used form of TF domestically and globally. It is important to understand that an AR is not a *loan* between the parties but is simply a legal claim for payment between a Seller and its Buyer. This distinction is important for understanding how risk mitigation and other financing tools apply differently to AR, loans, and other forms of TF debt.

---

2 The term "sale" can also refer to various parts of the sales process, including a sales pitch, sales meetings, sales agreement, sales delivery, and ultimately, sales execution.

Invoices

Invoices are a Seller's billing notice to its Buyer in the form of a statement outlining its claim for payment. An Invoice is not an AR, even though many TF practitioners incorrectly use the terms AR and Invoice interchangeably. Nevertheless, Invoices contain various transaction details and can serve as good evidence of an AR, and they may be used by accountants, payment processors, or tax, customs, and other authorities to record or review relevant parts of a Trade.

Trade Currency

TF can be conducted in any currency agreed to by the transaction parties. Custom and practice, and the desire to use stable and easily convertible currencies, result in most TF using US Dollars or Euros and, to a lesser extent, other currencies such as Japanese Yen or British Pounds. Domestic TF, however, will generally use the currency of the country in which the Trade is executed. If given the choice, a Buyer would prefer to do TF business in the currency in which it generates most of its revenue. Otherwise, it will bear the risk of losses caused by declines in the value of its revenue currency relative to the value of its Trade Currency.

Trade Debt

Trade Debt is an Obligor's obligation to pay its Financier within a specific period of time to finance a Buyer's Trade. The most common form of Trade Debt is a Buyer's obligation to pay its Seller its AR within the period of time allowed it after delivery of its Items. However, Trade Debt can also take other forms, such as promissory notes, Bills of Exchange, loans, or a Buyer's reimbursement obligations to pay its Letter of Credit provider. Each form of Trade Debt has unique characteristics that can affect how suitable it is to meet the needs or structure of a TF transaction.

Trade Payables

Trade Payables are a Buyer's legal obligation to pay its Seller's AR. Trade Payables are recorded as liabilities on the Buyer's accounting books and records. Trade Payables are not accounted for as secured debt, and, therefore, generally do not affect any secured borrowing restrictions the Buyer may have agreed to with other creditors. This accounting feature makes the use of payables appealing in Supply Chain and Confirmed Payables Financing, which is explained further in Chapter 4.

TF MECHANICS

Credit Terms

Credit Terms are the conditions under which an Obligor is obligated to pay its Trade Debt to its Financier. Credit Terms, at a minimum, define the financed amounts, payment schedules, interest rates, fees, and any other charges. They may also include any discounts or penalties for early or late payment, and other special conditions.

Credit Amounts

Credit Amounts are the amount of funds a Financier agrees to provide, or put at risk, in a transaction. The Credit Amount may be for up to 100% of the Buyer's Items' cost plus additional financing, legal, or other "closing" costs. In many cases, other than Seller-provided Credit Terms in the form of its AR, Credit Amounts will typically be for less than 100% of the Buyers Item's cost because Financiers will often require the Buyer to make a partial "advance" or "down" payment (e.g., 10% of the Trade amount) to the Seller to ensure that the Buyer has funds at risk in the transaction, or has some "skin in the game" as some Financiers like to say. A Buyer, on the other hand, will typically desire, and try to negotiate, the highest possible Credit Amount relative to its Trade amount in order to minimize its use of its working capital.

Credit Periods

A Credit Period is the length of time, measured by days, months, or years, by which a Trade Debt is required to be paid in accordance with its Credit Terms. In the case of AR, the Credit Period is the number of days by which the Buyer is required to pay its Seller (e.g., 30 days or more). In the case of any other form of Trade Debt, the Credit Period is the length of time in which the Obligor is required to pay its Financier as agreed and stated in its Trade Debt agreement. Credit Periods normally fall into three categories: short-term generally means 30, 60, or exceptionally 90 to 180 days; medium-term generally means 1 to 5 years, typically to be paid down with semi-annual or quarterly principal and interest payments; and long-term generally means 5 to 12 years, typically to be paid down with semi-annual or quarterly principal and interest payments. Credit Periods generally do not exceed the useful life of the Items being financed. Medium- and long-term Credit Periods from 5 to 12 years, for example, are generally used for capital goods Items (e.g., large machines, ships, airplanes), which typically require a number of years to generate sufficient revenue to enable the Obligor to pay down the related Trade Debt.

Credit Advances

Credit Advances, which are also sometimes referred to as "disbursements" or "draws," occur each time a Financier delivers, or puts at risk, funds to pay a Seller on behalf of its Buyer or other Obligor. Credit Advances are made in accordance with the Financier's Trade Debt agreement (usually a loan, Promissory Note, or other instrument) with its Obligor. For example, a Financier that has agreed to issue a $1,000,000 loan to an Obligor to finance a Buyer's purchase of Items from its Seller may, at the time the Items are delivered, make a $1,000,000 Credit Advance to the Seller on behalf of and at the Borrower's request. Alternatively, if the Items are to be delivered in a series of deliveries made over a period of time, the Financier may make a series of smaller Credit Advances at the time of each delivery until all its Credit Advances eventually add up to the $1,000,000 Credit Amount.

Credit Facility

A Credit Facility, which may also be referred to as a "credit line," is a Financier's commitment to make Credit Advances, up to an agreed aggregate maximum Credit Amount, to an Obligor over an agreed time period (the "Credit Facility Validity Period"), which is usually for a period of one year or less. Each Credit Advance will be required to be repaid within the agreed Credit Period (e.g., 30, 60, or 90 days, or 1 year or longer). If the Credit Facility is a *revolving* one, the Borrower may reborrow any Credit Amounts it has repaid during the Credit Facility Validity Period. The Financier's legal commitment to make Credit Advances is typically subject to modification or cancellation by the Financier if it determines that its Obligor's credit condition or other market conditions have materially changed. An alternative to a committed Credit Facility is a "guidance" Credit Facility, in which the Financier has no legal commitment to make Credit Advances but may do so at its sole discretion.

Interest

Financiers earn interest from Obligors based on their interest rate, which is composed of the Financier's funding costs, based on its cost of capital or debt it uses for funding transactions, and its "Margin," based on its perceived Credit and other risks, the scarcity of credit available for a particular Obligor, competitive pressures, the price other Financiers charge this or similar Obligors, and the degree to which the Trade Debt can be easily transferred (its liquidity) to other Financiers in case the Financier wants to exit or share the Trade Debt. For example, a Financier with a cost of funds of 2% per annum that charges a Margin equal to 1% per annum, results in a total interest rate of 3% per annum. A Financier's cost of funds may fluctuate day-to-day, based on market conditions and its ability to obtain funds at stable rates. A Financier's Margin, however, should remain fixed unless the parties renegotiate it due to a change in Credit or transaction risks.

Interest Periods

Interest is charged at a fixed or variable per annum rate for the duration of the Trade Debt's Credit Period and is paid at the end ("in arrears") or the beginning ("in advance") of each periodic monthly, quarterly, semi-annual, or annual Interest Period. An interest rate may be called a "discount rate" if the Financier calculates and collects its interest in *advance* of each Interest Period in the form of a deduction from each of its Credit Advances. This is often the case, for example, in AR Purchase Finance transactions, discussed in detail in Chapter 4, in which the Financier typically collects its interest at the time it purchases the AR by deducting it from the Seller's AR proceeds.

Each interest payment is calculated for the number of days in each Interest Period for which the Credit Amount is outstanding and unpaid. For example, a $12,000,000 loan being repaid over a Credit Period of 1 year in 12 equal monthly principal payments has 12 Interest Periods for which either a variable interest rate will be set at the beginning of each Interest Period or a fixed interest rate will apply to each Interest Period.

Fixed interest or discount rates are used for AR Purchases, and for some medium- and long-term transactions, with structures that are suitable for fixed interest rates. Most other Trade Debt, however, is funded using variable, or "floating," interest rates that can change throughout the duration of the Trade Debt's Credit Period.

Amortization

Amortization is the manner and schedule by which a Trade Debt is paid down during its Credit Period. Amortization methods and schedules used in TF are a function of industry standards and the parties' agreement. Short-term Trade Debt, such as 30-day AR, is typically paid down in a single lump-sum "bullet" payment 30 days after an Item's delivery. Other short-term Trade Debt may be amortized in a series of monthly principal and interest payments until the end of its Credit Period.

Medium- and long-term Trade Debt typically amortizes in equal quarterly or semi-annual *principal* installments, resulting in a consistent decline in the outstanding principal Trade Debt amount. Interest is calculated on the outstanding and yet unpaid principal balance, payable in advance as a discount or in arrears on each scheduled principal payment date.

Alternatively, for some long-term Trade Debt, for which fixed and equal scheduled payment amounts may be required, "mortgage-style" amortization may be used. For this type of amortization, the *combined* total amount of each principal installment and interest payment remains the same throughout the Credit Period. This is accomplished by having the principal installment amounts due increase over time, while the accompanying interest amounts due decrease over time. Mortgage-style amortization also requires that a fixed rate of interest be established and applied to the Trade Debt from its beginning in order to establish a fixed series of periodic, equal principal and interest payments throughout the Credit Period. Mortgage-style amortization carries more risk for the Financier because it allows most of its principal Credit Amount to be repaid later in the Credit Period, and it carries the risk that in the event of an uncured payment default, early termination resulting in fixed interest rate breakage costs may occur (discussed in Chapter 5). The parties will also typically agree to use mortgage-style amortization when the Trade Debt is structured as a Financed Lease, which typically requires equal periodic principal and interest payments to make them appear to tax and legal authorities as periodic "rental" payments rather loan repayments. Otherwise, if the lease structure is challenged and the transaction is determined by the relevant authorities to be a form of debt, rather than a lease, the parties' legal relationships would change, which could have adverse legal and accounting consequences.

Average Life

A Trade Debt's Average Life, refers to the average amount of time, measured in years or fractions thereof, during which the Credit Amount is outstanding, unpaid, and at risk during its Credit Period. For example, a Trade Debt that is to be fully funded on day one and to be repaid in one single bullet payment in five years has a five-year Average Life. However, if that same Trade Debt is to be repaid in ten equal semi-annual principal installments, its Average Life would be only 2.75 years, because the amount of its outstanding and unpaid principal Credit Amount declines over its five-year Credit Period, thus reducing the time during which its principal Credit Amount is at risk. Taking into account a Trade Debt's Average Life is important for accurately assessing Credit and other risks, and for determining appropriate pricing, because it reflects the actual duration and amount of a Financier's risk during a Credit Period. In the example above, the 5-year loan repayable in a single bullet payment, with an Average Life of 5 years, carries more risk than the 5-year amortizing loan with an Average Life of 2.75 years. A loan's Average Life is calculated by dividing (a) the sum of each weighted periodic principal repayment expressed as a percentage of the principal repaid relative to each scheduled repayment date by (b) the total amount of all principal repayments.

Example: $10 mm[3] fully drawn loan, amortizing in 10 equal semi-annual periodic principal repayments:

A	B	C = (AxB)
Semi-Annual Repayments over 5 Years	10 Semi-Annual Repayments Amounts	% of Principal Repayments paid Relative to each Payment Date
0.5	$1,000,000	$500,000
1	$1,000,000	$1,000,000
1.5	$1,000,000	$1,500,000
2	$1,000,000	$2,000,000
2.5	$1,000,000	$2,500,000
3.0	$1,000,000	$3,000,000
3.5	$1,000,000	$3,500,000
4.0	$1,000,000	$4,000,000
4.5	$1,000,000	$4,500,000
5	$1,000,000	$5,000,000
Totals:	$10,000,000	$27,500,000

C/B ($27,500,000/$10,000,000) = 2.75 Years Average Loan Life

Fees

A Financier may charge fees to compensate it for various services, such as transaction execution and administration, or fees can simply be a source for additional income. Fees are typically called Arranging, Agent, Servicing, Discount, Legal, Administrative, Facility, and Disbursement Fees.

For example, the Financier may charge an up-front transaction setup fee (e.g., called a "facility fee" or "arrangement fee") equal to 1% of the Credit Amount. It may also charge a commitment fee equal to some percentage (e.g., 1%) of the unused Credit Amount, calculated and payable monthly in advance or arrears. Agency Fees may

---

3   In finance, mm is a common abbreviation for million.

be charged in cases where an Agent (usually the Financier or a third-party agency specialist) is needed to perform a transaction monitoring and coordination role among a group of Financiers that are cooperating on a single transaction.

TF LEGAL AGREEMENTS & DOCUMENTATION

Most countries' laws will allow transaction parties to agree to whatever TF terms and conditions they want, on the condition they do not violate applicable local laws, regulations, or some public policy. Local laws or regulations (such as "Sale of Goods" statutes, which have been enacted in many jurisdictions) may add, modify, or limit a transaction party's obligations, rights, or risks in a transaction, even if those laws or regulations are not referenced or incorporated in the parties' transaction agreements. For example, in many countries, selling nonconforming goods will give rise to a legitimate Trade Dispute and will nullify or dilute the Seller's right to payment, without the need for the parties' transaction agreement to expressly provide this defense. Another example are laws prohibiting the sale of contraband or regulated Items, or transactions with officially sanctioned parties, from being enforceable, regardless of the parties' agreements to the contrary.

Since most TF is domestic, not international, the laws of the parties' country, or one of its legal subdivisions (e.g., States or Regions), will in most cases govern how their transactions are documented and enforced. For international TF, the laws of either the Buyer's or Seller's country or one of its legal subdivisions, may be selected by the parties to govern their transaction. Frequently, international TF transactions (particularly the larger ones) are governed by either US (New York) law or English law and provide for enforcement through New York's or England's courts—even if the Buyer and Seller are not incorporated in the US or the UK.

For some domestic or international transactions, an internationally recognized set of rules may be selected or incorporated into the TF Agreement when they are better suited for a particular transaction or provide specific legal protections to one or more of the transaction parties that would not be available in their countries. For example, most Letter of Credit transactions will incorporate by reference the current and applicable Uniform Customs and Practices for Documentary Credits (UCP) to govern that Letter of Credit.

Despite the fact that any number of laws could govern TF transactions domestically or internationally, it is nevertheless useful for understanding how laws can affect how TF is conducted by providing a summary of the basic legal principles used in the United States because it generates a good deal of domestic and international TF.

Agreements — Contracts

Legally binding and enforceable TF agreements can be created verbally or be documented in writing, including by means of electronic communications and records. Because it is generally easier to enforce and operate written or electronically recorded agreements, most TF transactions are recorded or documented in writing with varying degrees of formality. Even AR, which generally do not require any written agreement among the parties, are aided in their operation and enforcement by supporting documents such as accounting records, Invoices, purchase orders, sales agreements, and delivery and transport documents.

A legally binding contract between parties typically requires, at a minimum, an offer, acceptance, and the exchange of consideration between parties with authority to enter into the contract. TF contracts involving large dollar amounts, medium- or long-term Credit Periods, or structuring features will generally be documented using formal sales, loan, credit, or other Trade Debt agreements and a host of accompanying documents to memorialize the transaction in sufficient detail to facilitate its ongoing administration. Oftentimes, the parties' sales teams, with input from legal advisors or product specialists, will negotiate and execute a TF Agreement and then, once executed, hand the agreement to another transaction implementation or operations team for further execution, servicing, and monitoring. Well-drafted transaction agreements and supporting documents should provide clear guidance for administering the transaction and describe the procedures for addressing potential disputes and enforcement.

TF Legal Agreements and their resulting Trade Debts are typically documented in the following ways.

Negotiable Trade Debt Instruments

Negotiable Trade Debt Instruments are written or digitally recorded instruments stating its Issuer's, and any co-issuer's or Guarantor's, absolute, unconditional, and freely transferrable promise to pay the instruments' original or subsequent owner. They are frequently used to document Trade Debt and commonly take the form of negotiable promissory notes, Bills of Exchange, or Drafts. They are legally enforceable by their own terms upon presentation to its Issuer, without the need for supplemental or supporting documentation or the satisfaction of external conditions. To be a Negotiable Trade Debt Instrument, a document must (a) be issued by a Buyer or other original Obligor (e.g., a Buyer's bank); (b) state the issuing party's, and any co-Issuer's or Guarantor's, irrevocable payment obligation of a certain amount, due by certain dates, upon presentation by the instrument's current owner to the Issuer; and (c) not contain any language that inhibits, restricts, or otherwise prevents the instrument's lawful transfer to another party. The transfer of Negotiable Trade Debt Instruments from the current owner (the legal "Holder") to another is typically done by means of Endorsement, which requires the Holder to sign ("endorse") the instrument to its new Holder without recourse. So long as the new Holder took the instrument in good faith and for value, it may generally qualify as a "Holder in Due Course." Any Holder in Due Course may enforce the instrument against the Issuer directly, without involving any previous Holder and free of most claims and defenses to payment. In many cases, it is desirable to use Negotiable Trade Debt

Instruments to make certain types of Trade Debt more easily transferable to access a greater pool of potential Financiers in order to improve pricing or credit capacity, or for other structuring reasons.

Bills of Exchange

Bills of Exchange are used in TF transactions to document Trade Debts in the form of Drafts. Drafts used for TF are written or digital instruments issued and delivered by a Seller (the Drawer of the Draft), instructing its Buyer (the Drawee under the Draft) or its designated Payor (e.g., the Buyer's bank) to make payment immediately (Sight Draft) or at some future date (Time Draft) to the payee named in the Draft. If the Buyer acknowledges and "Accepts" on the Draft that it is legally obligated to pay represented debt, the Draft becomes a Negotiable Trade Debt Instrument. Once the Draft becomes negotiable, the payee named in the Draft, (e.g., the Seller), may sell it to any other Financier by Endorsement, generally making that subsequent Financier a Holder in Due Course. Any Holder in Due Course may simply present the Draft to the Buyer, or its designated Payor, demanding payment. Accepted Drafts have the following features:

a) The Buyer, or its designated Payor, waives any defense of payment for any reason, as the obligation to pay is independent of the underlying trade and therefore not affected by a Trade Dispute.

b) Drafts are freely transferrable to other parties by Endorsement or other lawful means of transfer (e.g., Assignment).

c) Holders in Due Course that have received the Negotiable Debt Instrument by means of *Endorsement without recourse* have no recourse to the Seller for any Buyer nonpayment unless the Draft is a product of fraud by the Seller or Buyer.

Example - Bill of Exchange Used for Cross-Border TF:

After a Seller delivers Items to its Buyer by ship, the Seller sends its Sight Draft to the Buyer, or to the Buyer's designated bank, accompanied by negotiable transport documents that give the Buyer (or its freight forwarder) the legal right to take possession of the Items at the delivery port. A negotiable bill of lading, or other negotiable transport document (airway bill or trucking bill of lading), is one that, in accordance with applicable laws, enables its Holder to take possession of the goods identified on that bill of lading. Negotiable cross-border transport documents will typically include the Seller's commercial invoice, the ship's (or other transport means) negotiable bill of lading, and a certificate of origin issued by a recognized authority, such as a chamber of commerce in the Seller's country, and any other certificates required by the Buyer or the port authorities (customs or tax) to enable the Buyer to take delivery.

Promissory Notes

Promissory Notes may be used to evidence a Trade Debt in which a Buyer, acting in its capacity as a Borrower and "Issuer," issues a Promissory Note to its payee/

Holder, which is the Seller or another Financier. If a Promissory Note states that its payment obligation is *absolute and unconditional* and subject only to demand or presentation to the Issuer, it becomes a Negotiable Trade Debt Instrument and can be freely transferred to other Holders without requiring permission from its Issuer. Promissory Notes represent their Issuer's debt obligations to pay the Holder a certain Credit Amount in one or more scheduled payments of principal, plus interest (if any). The Issuer's Guarantor, if any, may also guarantee payment of the Promissory Note to the Holder. The Guarantee will be stated directly on the Promissory Note or in a separate Guarantee document.

At a minimum, Promissory Notes should identify the Issuer (Buyer or Borrower) by name and address, the payee, date of issuance, amount due, payment schedule, and interest due, if any. When payment is due, the payee presents the Promissory Note to the Issuer for immediate payment. If a Promissory Note contains language that conditions payment on the satisfaction of certain conditions or references other agreements that govern its payment obligations, it is not a Negotiable Trade Debt Instrument and thus operates merely as supplemental documentation or information supporting the Issuer's related Trade Debt agreement.

Example - Promissory Note as Negotiable Trade Debt Instrument:

A Buyer agrees to Issue a Promissory Note in which it unconditionally promises to pay the Financier or any subsequent Holder $1,000,000, plus interest at 5% p.a. 12 months from its issuance date. In exchange for the Promissory Note, the Financier agrees to pay the Seller $1,000,000, on behalf of the Buyer, for its Items. After 12 months, the Buyer pays the Financier $1,050,000.

Loan Agreements

Loan Agreements, which may also be referred to as Credit Agreements or Facility Agreements, are commonly used to document medium- or long-term Trade Debts between a Buyer, or a Borrower or Guarantor acting on its behalf, and a Financier, acting in its capacity as the Lender. A Seller is not normally a party to a TF Loan Agreement unless it is providing, in its capacity as a Lender, the loan directly to its Buyer. The purpose of a Loan and the relevant Sellers to which the Lender will be disbursing loan funds will typically be mentioned in the Loan Agreement. Loan Agreements are useful for documenting more complex borrowing arrangements, which may include numerous restrictions and conditions that must be continually satisfied to justify ongoing loan disbursements or to avoid the loan's early termination. Lenders using a Loan Agreement will also typically require legal opinions from the Lender's and Borrower's attorneys confirming that the Loan Agreement is legally valid and enforceable in the jurisdiction in which the parties do business, and that it has been executed in accordance with the Borrower's internal governing rules (e.g., bylaws) and is signed by one or more individuals authorized to represent the Borrower.

Term Sheets

The manner and form in which a TF Agreement is documented also affects the parties' legal costs and the time and effort needed to negotiate and execute a transaction. Except for creating AR in the normal course of a Seller's business, parties intending to enter into a TF Agreement will typically initiate their TF negotiations with a Term Sheet that summarizes their proposed Credit Terms and other conditions, which they intend to later memorialize with appropriate legally binding documentation. Term Sheets themselves, however, are generally not legally binding contracts and will typically state they are "indicative" and "nonbinding." Every Term Sheet from a credible Financier, however, carries with it a presumption that it is made with the good faith intention and, in some legal jurisdictions, with varying degrees of legal obligation, that the proposed terms can be delivered barring unforeseen or unknown circumstances, or unless specific *material* conditions stated in the Term Sheet are not satisfied by the parties. This good faith presumption typically requires a Financier to conduct some level of internal credit, risk, compliance, and legal due diligence before providing a Term Sheet to a prospective client.

Fee Letters

Financiers commonly memorialize their fee agreements with their Obligors in a separate agreement, typically referred to as a Fee Letter, rather than in their Trade Debt agreements. This allows the parties to keep their fee arrangements confidential and to disclose them only to those it chooses. Fee Letters are especially useful when Trade Debt is sold or shared among Financiers in order to avoid disclosing the arranging or lead Financier's earned fees.

CHAPTER 2

Trade Finance Risks

The key risks in most TF transactions usually involve one or more transaction parties failing to honor their payment, delivery, performance, or legal obligations, or changes in laws or market conditions that lead to those results. The most common examples include a Buyer not paying for its Items due to its temporary or permanent financial inability, a Seller not delivering the Items as promised, and changes in laws that prevent a party from honoring its obligations or benefiting from its transaction. The transaction parties that bear each of these risks are determined according to their TF transaction structures, legal agreements, and applicable laws.

Structuring TF involves identifying and allocating transaction risks to the parties that are best suited to taking them, and where possible, utilizing appropriate and cost-effective risk-mitigating products and solutions. TF risks can be categorized by type, as explained below, and are often interconnected and overlapping. For example, the risk of a law changing that increases the cost of a transaction or makes it illegal to complete or enforce can be labeled as a legal, commercial, or political risk. Similarly, currency or debt collateral devaluation can be labeled either an economic or commercial risk, which may in turn result in currency transfer restrictions imposed by a government, which can be termed a political risk. Despite these overlaps, it is important to identify and distinguish these various risks as precisely as possible in order to address and possibly mitigate their effects using the available TF risk mitigation tools and solutions described further below.

Credit Risk

Credit Risk is the risk that a transaction party becomes *financially unable* to honor its financial obligations and is often the primary risk to identify and address in a TF transaction. Credit Risk usually focuses on assessing whether a Buyer or Obligor is "creditworthy," which means it has the financial ability to honor all of its debt obligations, including its TF ones. However, Credit Risks can also pertain to other transaction parties, which might become insolvent (bankrupt) or may experience temporary cash flow shortages. For example, a Seller's Credit Risk may be that it runs short of funds and become unable to deliver promised Items or to honor its warranty or other obligations to the Buyer. A Financier's Credit Risk may be that it is or becomes financially weak or insolvent to the point that it is unable to honor its commitment to provide or put at risk funds for its transactions. For example, if a Financier has agreed to use a funding benchmark, such as the London Interbank Bank Rate (LIBOR) or SOFR, and its financial condition weakens, that Financier may lose its ability to fund itself at that rate. Similarly, if a third-party Guarantor's or TC Insurer's financial condition weakens, it could lose its ability to honor its financial obligations to pay claims.

Credit Risk assessments can take several forms, including analyzing the relevant party's financial statements; reviewing its actual debt payment history as reported by itself, other creditors, or credit reporting companies; or assessing alternative credit data that may be available. Whatever methods or resources used, the Credit Risk analysis should be tailored to the specific contemplated TF transaction and its particular structure and risk profile. For example, a Buyer that operates in a volatile industry may not be creditworthy for a one-year, $1 mm Trade Debt, but it might be creditworthy for a 30-day, $5 mm Trade Debt that would be liquidated by its sale of Items to a long-term creditworthy Buyer under a fixed-price Trade agreement.

Trade Disputes

Trade Disputes occur when a Buyer or Seller claims that the other party failed to honor one or more terms of their Trade agreement. For example, a Buyer may refuse to pay for all or part of the delivered Items, claiming they do not conform to the parties' Trade agreement, and the Seller disputes the Buyer's claim of nonconformity. For example, a Seller delivers 10 sky blue uniforms to the Buyer. However, the Buyer claims it ordered 10 navy blue uniforms, the color of which was shown to the Buyer in the Seller's catalogue, and the purchase order did not state exactly which blue was being ordered. Accordingly, the Buyer refuses to pay the Seller due to this Trade Dispute. Another example of a Trade Dispute may occur when a Seller refuses to honor its warranty or delivery obligations in a timely manner for some reason the Buyer disputes. Trade Disputes are generally resolved through negotiation or litigation.

Commercial Risk

Commercial Risk is a broad term referring to economic events (e.g., recessions, or market or supply chain disruptions) or actions taken by a transaction party that may prevent one or more of the parties from honoring their payment or other transaction obligations. Commercial Risks can include Trade Disputes among a Seller, Buyer, or other transaction party, including third-party guarantors or TC Insurers or Financiers. Other Commercial Risks include a Buyer cancelling a sales agreement after the Seller has invested funds to fulfill an order, or the devaluation of currency, collateral, or other security used in a transaction, which may or may not result in a Credit Risk. A Buyer's refusal to pay the Seller for non-financial reasons (e.g., delivery of nonconforming Items) is both a Trade Dispute and a Commercial Risk, but it is not a Credit Risk.

Economic Risk

Economic Risks include events or conditions that can disrupt one or more economies, such as inflation, recession, commodity price volatility, natural disasters, and pandemics, in ways that make a TF transaction difficult or impossible to execute. Economic Risks and their causes and effects are often difficult or impossible to predict. They may result in Financiers and other transaction parties suddenly becoming insolvent or transactions suddenly becoming legally prohibited or prohibitively expensive.

Legal and Regulatory Risk

Legal and Regulatory Risks include the application, introduction, or revision of a law or regulation that unexpectedly prevents one or more transaction parties' ability to execute a TF transaction as it was intended or causes the transaction to become uneconomical for one or more of the parties. Examples include revocation of business licenses, changes in laws or regulations that result in a transaction being deemed illegal or unenforceable, imposition of monetary transfer or currency exchange restrictions, changes in bank regulatory capital requirements, or changes to tax or accounting laws. To address some of these risks, TF parties will typically try to have their transactions governed by laws and judicial systems that are the most stable, predictable, and favorable to their interests.

Political Risk

Political Risks include government actions or government-related events outside the transaction parties' control that can prevent a TF transaction from being executed as planned or that prevents a transaction party from being able to honor its financial or other obligations. Examples of Political Risks include war, civil unrest, or government actions that lead to business or asset expropriation; seizure of businesses or collateral or other security; impositions of new laws that restrict the transfer of funds or foreign currency exchange; embargoes; or government or publicly owned companies refusing to honor their contracts or their judicial or arbitral decisions.

Compliance Risk

Compliance Risks include a transaction party failing to comply with applicable laws or regulations, which may result in penalties or other enforcement actions or restrictions on its ability to execute or benefit from a TF transaction. Examples include national or international sanctions violations, unfair lending practices, breach of privacy laws, participating knowingly or unknowingly in money laundering activities, or other illegal transactions.

Operational Risk

Operational Risks include a transaction party failing to execute its operational or administrative obligations, which is often the result of unintentional human or mechanical errors. Examples include, a Financier not delivering funds or the correct amount to another party on time due to a breakdown within its payment systems, or a Buyer not being able to take delivery of goods on time due to transportation or logistics failures, or one of the transaction parties failing to take actions or to deliver documents or Items due to its error, omission, or negligence.

Funding Risk

Funding Risks include a Financier being unable or unwilling to fund its transaction at agreed interest rates during all or part of the transaction due its own insolvency, regulatory or legal changes, or disruption in the credit markets. Massive disruption in the credit markets occurred following the 2008 financial crisis, which dramatically increased short-term interest rates for a period of time. Other funding risks may involve an Obligor voluntarily or involuntarily repaying its Trade Debt earlier than the end of its Credit Period, potentially causing interest rate breakage costs to be paid by it or its Financier.

Fraud Risk

Fraud Risk includes one or more parties intentionally misrepresenting itself or providing false or misleading information to another party to achieve financial or other gain. Fraud is committed by businesses of all sizes and in all geographies. These companies will typically do their utmost to appear legitimate on the surface to hide or disguise their fraudulent activities. A common example of TF fraud occurs when Sellers or Buyers engage in fictitious Trades designed to defraud Financiers, or Trades involving fictitious Invoices designed to defraud tax, customs, or other authorities. Financiers can commit fraud by taking bribes to provide exceptional or non-market Credit Terms, launder money, do business with sanctioned parties, or finance illegal Trades (e.g., sanctioned or contraband goods).

CHAPTER 3

TF Risk Mitigation Tools

The most commonly used TF risk mitigation tools are explained below. Each of these can become complex, varied, and nuanced enough to justify an entire book being written about it. Nevertheless, the explanations of the tools in this material are designed to provide a functional guide and understanding for how and when they may be used to mitigate particular TF risks. It is important to understand that not all TF risks can be cost-effectively mitigated or reduced to zero, and that there are costs to using them in terms of price, time, and effort. In many, if not most transactions, TF risks are simply assessed, accepted without mitigation, and assigned to the transaction party most willing and able to afford them. For example, the vast majority of TF used in the world, Seller to Buyer AR finance, is carried on with little or no risk mitigation tools or structures.

TRADE CREDIT INSURANCE (TCI)

Trade Credit Insurance (TCI) covers the risk of an Obligor's (usually a Buyer or Borrower) nonpayment of its Trade Debt due its financial inability to pay, which may be evidenced by it entering into legally recognized insolvency proceedings (e.g., bankruptcy filing) or by its prolonged payment default lasting approximately 60 or more days. TCI has become one of the most used TF risk mitigation tools for both Sellers and other Financiers and can be applied to cover just about every type of Trade Debt. TCI may be purchased by a Seller or Financier from a TC Insurer, which is also referred to in the TF industry as a "carrier" or "underwriter." TCI is sold by over 50 private TC Insurers globally and by some ECAs and other organizations, and is estimated to generate approximately $10 billion in annual premiums paid by insureds.[4] TCI is used more widely throughout Europe than in the US,

---

4   According to Allied Market Research's "2021 Trade Credit Insurance Market" report by Aarti Goswami, Pramod Borasi, Vineet Kumar. The global trade credit insurance market size was valued at $9.39 billion in 2019 and is projected to reach $18.14 billion by 2027, growing at a CAGR of 8.6% from 2020 to 2027. https://www.alliedmarketresearch.com/trade-credit-insurance-market-A08305

Another projection by Valuates Reports estimates the global Credit Insurance Market size to reach $13.6 billion by 2026, from $12.0 billion in 2020, at a CAGR of 2.1% during 2021–2026. https://reports.valuates.com/market-reports/ALLI-Auto-4K411/trade-credit-insurance

but is growing in popularity in the US and Asia as it becomes better understood and trusted.

Sellers are by far the largest purchasers of TCI, using it to cover all or some of their Buyers' AR nonpayment risks. Other Financiers use TCI to cover their Trade Debts, including loans or a Buyer's nonpayment of AR that the Financiers purchase from Sellers. Political Risks can also be covered under a TCI or separate Political Risk Insurance contract. TC Insurers agree to pay the insured party a percentage, generally ranging from 80% to 90%, of the insured's unpaid Trade Debt arising from specifically named Obligors, Buyers, or Borrowers. To cover a Seller's large multi-Buyer portfolio of AR, TCI can cover unspecified Buyers that meet certain pre-agreed "discretionary credit limit" criteria. TC Insurers pay claims to their insured after a pre-agreed "waiting period" has expired, which is typically 30 to 180 days after the insured loss has occurred or a claim was filed.

TCI does not cover losses due to Trade Disputes, AR Dilution, or fraud, or in cases where the insured fails to satisfy conditions of the TCI Contract. TCI is *not* a payment Guarantee, with the key difference being that TCI is conditional and requires the insured to "prove" its loss and that it has satisfied all the terms of the TCI Contract. In contrast, an unconditional payment Guarantee simply requires nonpayment of the guaranteed debt and that timely demand be made on the Guarantor, regardless as to whether the Trade or Trade Debt obligation is disputed.

TCI Benefits

Sellers

- Cover losses due to a Buyer's nonpayment of AR.
- Cover losses caused by Political Risks.
- Cover pre-delivery production costs for cancelled orders.
- Increase sales and competitiveness by expanding the number of Buyers to which it can offer Credit Terms.
- Improve Buyer Credit Risk management, compliance processes, and sales strategies by using TC Insurer–provided credit data and analysis about existing or potential Buyers.
- Reduce operational costs by outsourcing all or part of its Credit Risk management to the TC Insurer.
- Increase loan advance rates from Asset-Based Lenders that give extra value to TC insured loan collateral.

Financiers

- Cover losses due to Obligor nonpayment.
- Grow TF business by taking on insured Credit Risks and leveraging risk appetite.

- Improve Credit Risk analysis by using credit reports and analysis provided by TC Insurers about existing or potential Obligors.

- Decrease the amount of regulatory capital Financiers are required to reserve for TF transactions when they allowed by their regulators to treat TCI as a financial Guarantee.

- Purchase large portfolios of AR from Sellers without having to analyze the creditworthiness of every single Buyer.

Buyers and Obligors
- Increase the number of Sellers and other Financiers that are willing to provide them Credit Terms. Obligors whose key Sellers and other Financiers rely significantly on the availability of TCI may engage directly with TC Insurers, make their financial information available to the TC Insurers, and address any potential credit or other concerns in order to encourage the TC Insurers to cover their risks.

TCI Contracts

Contracts
Contracts are typically valid for one year and are composed of multiple components, including the insured's Application for Insurance, Policy, Declaration Page, and if needed, Endorsements that amend the standard policy terms. These components may take different forms and may be called different names, depending on the country in which they are used. For example, in some countries, the policy may be referred to as the "contract." Endorsements or other contract amendments or supplemental terms may be called "clauses," "riders," or "specificities." It is also important to understand that TCI is a heavily regulated industry in most countries, resulting in very specific rules TC Insurers must follow. Regulation can apply to the types of coverage TC Insurers can offer, their coverage terms, pricing, contract documentation, and underwriting methodology. In the United States, for example, each of its 50 States and the District of Columbia applies its own unique TCI regulations to any TC Insurer doing business in that State or District or that provides TCI to insureds in that State or District. Accordingly, TCI documentation, terms, and practice may vary greatly throughout the world, and a TC Insurer's range of flexibility as to how it conducts business will be greatly affected and restricted by its national or local laws and regulations.

Applications
Applications for TC Insurance are made by a prospective insured either directly to the TC Insurer or to the TC Insurer's Agent or through the prospective insured's Broker. A TC Insurer's completed Application is typically required as a condition to issuing the TC Insurance Contract. However, as a practical matter, the Application is usually preceded with a simple request for a quote to the TC Insurer, in which enough basic information (e.g., names of Buyers or Obligors and requested

Credit Limits) will be submitted to enable the TC Insurer to produce a meaningful quote. In the United States, the Application is usually the only document the insured will countersign with the TC Insurer. The formal Application form will request information about the insured's business, the Trade Debts it wants covered, and, if the insured is a Seller or a Financier that is planning to purchase AR from a Seller, a list of its top ten Buyers, based on annual sales volumes, that includes their respective industries, places of business, and their payment histories in the form of an AR aging report that shows the payment status of outstanding Invoices, including past due Invoices, and the number of days payments typically remain outstanding (DSO). Obligor financial statements, if available, will be provided to the TC Insurer to aid its credit analysis and underwriting process. The Application and accompanying information submitted by the applicant will become a component of the final TCI Contract. Accordingly, the TC Insurer may later use any information in the Application that proved false or misleading to deny a claim. Applications, however, are not always required by TC Insurers, especially when they are renewing existing TCI Contracts. However, using the Application and keeping their information updated is generally a good practice that can lead to a better-informed credit analysis and underwriting process.

Policies

Policies state the basic terms of the insurance coverage, including definitions for coverage, losses, exclusions, waiting periods, claims procedures, and the parties' representations and warranties. A TC Insurer's standard policy language as well as any amendments needs to be approved and recorded with its regulators and therefore may remain unchanged for a number of years.

Endorsements

Endorsements are used to amend or add terms to the TC Insurer's standard policy language in order to customize an insured's coverage.

Declarations Pages

Declarations Pages typically appear as a cover page to the Policy and "declares" information specific to that TCI Contract, including the names and business locations of the insured, Indemnity and Co-Insurance Rates, Deductibles, Policy Period, Obligor Credit Limits, and other information that will vary from one TCI Contract to another.

Premiums and Insured's Costs

TC Insurers will charge the insured an annual premium to compensate it for the risks it covers. It may also charge up-front or recurring fees and sometimes its share of costs for recovered losses. Premiums for one-year TCI Contracts are normally due and payable at the time the TCI Contract becomes effective. Some Insurers may grant creditworthy insureds some time to pay the premium (e.g., 30 or more days) to improve their competitiveness. A TCI Insurer can deny claims if the insured has failed to pay its premium. Premiums may be calculated in the following ways:

4) **Sales based:** A percentage rate (e.g., 1%) calculated on the insured's projected insurable annual sales, to be updated and calculated quarterly or at year-end according to its actual annual sales. This method is typical when the insured is a Seller with a TCI Contract that covers most or all of its Obligors.

5) **Credit Limit based:** A percentage rate calculated on the aggregate amount of the insured's covered Credit Limits. This method is typical when a Financier is insuring loans or ongoing AR Purchases. For example, if a Financier is committed to purchase up to $10 mm of AR from a Seller for 1 year, it would require a covered Credit Limit of $10 mm and would therefore be charged a rate of 1% per annum on $10 mm (premium = $100,000).

6) **Usage based.** A percentage rate calculated on the actual amount of coverage used during the TCI Contract's Validity Period as determined by the insured. For example, if the insured is provided insured Credit Limits totaling $1 mm for an Obligor at a usage rate of 1% per annum, and the insured makes a 1-year loan to covered Obligors for only $500,000, the premium would be calculated at 1% per annum on only $500,000 (premium = $50,000).

For TCI Contracts with durations over one year, for example for medium-term loans, the premium may be collected in installments on a quarterly, yearly, or other basis. However, it is important to know that if an insured loss occurs prior to the end of the TCI Contract's period, the uncollected premium for the remainder of the Contract period is still due to the TC Insurer. For example, if a Financier makes a 5-year, $5 mm loan to an Obligor to finance its Trade, for which it is being charged a premium of 10% flat based on five years of insured risk (e.g., total premium of $500,000, payable annually in $100,000 installments), and the covered Obligor defaults after one year and is unable to repay any of the $5 mm loan, the Financier will still be obligated to pay the TC Insurer the full $500,000 of premium, not merely the first year's premium of $100,000.

Fees

TC Insurers may charge fees to cover their cost of underwriting and administering their TCI Contracts. A TC Insurer may charge either a flat underwriting fee based on a percentage of the total premium amount or a per Obligor underwriting fee for each Obligor it agrees to cover.

Recovery costs

Once a claim is paid, the TC Insurer may seek to recover its losses from the non-paying Obligor. The Insurance Contract and applicable laws or regulations will determine how any recoveries and related costs may be shared with the insured.

Common TCI Contract Terms

Indemnity Rate

Indemnity Rate is the *percentage* of an insured loss that the TC Insurer agrees to pay (*indemnify*) its insured. The insured bears the risk for any remaining percentage of loss (the insured's "Co-insurance rate"). Most TCI Contracts have Indemnity Rates covering 90% or 95% of the principal value of the insured debt, but higher or lower Indemnity Rates may be negotiated depending on the quality of the risk and transaction structure. For example, TCI with an Indemnity Rate of 90%, covering nonpayment of a $100 Trade Debt, will result in the TC Insurer paying a claim in the amount of $90 to its insured.

Co-Insurance

Co-Insurance is a form of risk sharing found in most TCI Contracts, whereby the insured shares some risk of loss with its TC Insurer. Risk sharing is intended to keep the insured active, involved, and motivated to minimize its and the TC Insurer's risk of loss. Risk sharing is typically done using Co-Insurance in which the insured shares a fixed percentage (e.g., 10%) of each loss with the TC Insurer, as would be reflected with an Indemnity Rate of, for example, 90%. The other common method of risk sharing is using a Deductible. Some TCI Contracts may use both Co-Insurance and a Deductible.

Deductible

A Deductible is the amount of one or more claimed losses the insured must sustain before the TC Insurer pays its share of any loss. TCI can impose either (a) an "aggregate first-loss Deductible," which is an amount equal to all the first losses sustained by the insured in aggregate for all covered Obligors; or (b) a "per Obligor Deductible" equal to a fixed percentage (e.g., 5%) of the first losses sustained by the Insured for *each covered Obligor*.

For example, if the TCI Contract has a 100% Indemnity Rate and a $20,000 *aggregate first-loss Deductible*, and the insured files a claim for an unpaid Trade Debt for $100,000, the TC Insurer will pay the insured $80,000 ($100,000 - $20,000 Deductible = $80,000). If that insured subsequently files another claim for $500,000 for losses resulting from unpaid Trade Debts owed by five different Obligors in the amounts of $100,000 each, the TC Insurer will pay the insured $500,000 because the $20,000 Deductible was already fully used up with insured's first claim.

If, on the other hand, the TCI Contract has an 100% Indemnity Rate and a 5% per Obligor Deductible, and an unpaid Trade Debt is owed by a single Obligor for $100,000, the Insurer will pay the insured $95,000. If that insured subsequently files another claim for $500,000 for losses resulting from unpaid Trade Debts owed by five different Obligors in the amounts of $100,000 each, the Insurer will pay the insured $475,000 after deducting the 5% ($5,000) Deductible from each Obligor loss.

If a TCI Contract includes both an aggregate first-loss Deductible (e.g., $20,000) and a Co-Insurance rate (e.g., 10%) and thus an 90% Indemnity Rate, a claim for a $100,000 unpaid Trade Debt will result in the TC Insurer paying its insured $72,000 ($100,000 loss - $20,000 Deductible = $80,000, minus 10% Co-Insurance ($8,000) = $72,000 claim payment. If this insured subsequently files another claim for a $100,000 loss, the TC Insurer will pay a claim in the amount of $90,000 ($100,000 - $10,000 Co-Insurance = $90,000).

Exclusions - What TCI Does Not Cover

Most TCI Contracts will expressly name excluded losses, the most common of which are those caused by the following:

- Fraud by either the Seller or Obligor.
- Insured's gross negligence, willful or wrongful acts, or omissions.
- Trade Disputes between Sellers and Obligors, unless the disputed amount is eventually settled by the parties or applicable legal authority.
- Insured's failure to disclose material information to the TC Insurer, which if disclosed, would have resulted in the TC Insurer denying coverage.
- Legal unenforceability of the underlying Trade Debt. TCI covers only Trade Debts that are legally enforceable. This condition, however, does not require that the Trade Debt be successfully enforced as a condition of coverage. Insured parties typically address this risk by obtaining legal opinions regarding the enforceability of their Trade Debt.
- Losses incurred during any war between any of the People's Republic of China, France, the United Kingdom, the Russian Federation, and/or the United States of America.
- Losses caused by nuclear war, nuclear accident, or radioactive contamination.

Cancellable vs. Non-Cancellable Coverage

TC Insurers may cancel or reduce coverage on one or more covered Obligors, unless the TCI Contract states that the coverage is non-cancellable. Obligor coverage cancellations or reductions may become effective immediately upon notice, or by a number of days after notice (e.g., 30 days or more). TC Insurers will typically reduce or cancel coverage when an Obligors' creditworthiness deteriorates or when economic or other risks rise for Obligors in certain industries or countries.

Some TC Insurers offer "non-cancellable" TCI Contracts. Others may agree to make specific Obligor Credit Limits non-cancellable, while leaving the rest cancellable. Non-cancellable TCI Contracts will typically come with conditions intended to prevent insureds from engaging in Trades or creating covered Trade Debt for which they have good reason to believe will not be paid. For example, a non-cancellable TCI Contract may require an insured Seller to "cease shipment" to Buyers that have insured AR that is past due by 60 days or more, or require Financiers to stop making loan disbursements or purchasing AR when they have reason to believe the covered Obligors will not pay their insured Trade Debt.

Loss Occurring vs. Loss Attaching Coverage

Most TCI Contracts are valid for one year ("Validity Period"), unless cancelled early by either party, and will provide either "Loss Occurring" or "Loss Attaching" coverage. Loss Occurring Contracts cover losses due to nonpayment of an insured Trade Debt that *originated* within the TCI Contract's Validity Period and *became past due* during that period. For example, for a Loss Occurring Insurance Contract that became effective January 1 with a Validity Period that ends December 31, in which the Obligor fails to pay its Trade Debt that originated on February 1 and was due on April 15, the loss will be covered because it both originated and became past due during the TCI Contract's Validity Period. If, however, that Trade Debt originated on December 15 and was not due for payment until January 15 of the succeeding year, that loss would not be covered because the debt became past due 15 days after the end of the TCI Contract's Validity Period.

Alternatively, Loss Attaching Insurance Contracts cover losses due to nonpayment of an insured Trade Debt that *originated* within the TCI Contract's Validity Period and became past due during that period or after it ended. For example, for a Loss Occurring Insurance Contract that became effective January 1 with a Validity Period that ends December 31, in which the Obligor fails to pay its Trade Debt that originated on December 15 but which did not become past due until January 15 of the succeeding year, the loss would be covered because coverage "attached" to the debt that *originated* during the TCI Contract's Validity Period.

Insured's Obligations to TC Insurer

The insured's obligations to the TC Insurer are stated in the TCI Contract. Fulfillment of those obligations by the insured is a condition of coverage, including the duty to take prompt actions to mitigate its losses. Those actions may include:

- A Seller ceasing shipments to a Buyer when the insured has reason to believe the Buyer may not pay its insured Trade Debt or when a covered Buyer is past due for a certain amount over a specified number of days.

- A Financier ceasing the purchase of AR payable by a Buyer that it has reason to believe may not pay its insured Trade Debt, or a Financier ceasing Credit Advances to an Obligor that it has reason to believe may not pay its insured Trade Debt.

- Reporting to the TC Insurer adverse information about a Buyer or other Obligor's business or financial condition that could reasonably be expected to affect its ability to pay its insured Trade Debt.

- Conducting a reasonable level of legal and compliance due diligence and sanctions screening to ensure its insured Trade Debt is legally binding and enforceable and not being used to support or hide criminal activity (e.g., money laundering, fraud, or sanctions violations).

- Refraining from taking actions that could reasonably be expected to adversely affect the TC Insurer's risks or its ability to recover losses (e.g., amending Trade Debt contracts that extend Credit Periods without the TC Insurer's prior permission).

- Making reasonable efforts during the post-claim "waiting period" (typically 30 to 180 days) to mitigate insured losses through negotiations, dialogue, or other recovery efforts approved by the TC Insurer.

How TC Insurers Underwrite Risks

Underwriting is the TC Insurer's process of analyzing an Obligor's creditworthiness and deciding whether to insure it and on what terms and conditions. Risk underwriting focuses on analyzing an Obligor's creditworthiness and other applicable risks (commercial, economic, or political) using available credit and business information, including financial statements, credit agency reports, and any available credit ratings. Based on its underwriting analysis, the TC Insurer will produce a list of Obligors and their respective Credit Limits representing the maximum amount of insured debt it is willing to cover for each Obligor. The underwriting process also identifies and excludes those Obligors it deems too risky to insure at any price. Commercial underwriting focuses on structuring the terms and conditions of coverage, including premiums, fees, Indemnity Rates, and risk sharing. Many, if not most, TC Insurers combine both risk and commercial underwriting into a single underwriting process, managed within a single underwriting department.

Access to reliable credit data and business information about Obligors is critical for TC Insurers to make informed decisions about which Obligors to insure and for determining their respective Credit Limits. Useful data includes up-to-date audited financial statements, AR or other debt payment histories, industry news and trends, as well as any other potentially relevant data that may inform underwriting decisions. Risk underwriting also analyzes the prospective insured's internal Credit Risk management process and its Obligor loss record. Most countries in the European Union have rules that require limited liability companies to make their financial statements publicly available by filing them with their respective national registries. This makes TCI underwriting for EU-registered Obligors quicker and less expensive than for those in other countries, most of which do not have such requirements. TC Insurers in the United States, by contrast, depend heavily on locally sourced credit reports from credit reporting businesses that provide only a very basic level of usable credit information for purposes of TCI underwriting.

Credit Ratings and Credit Scores

Some TC Insurers will use the results of their credit analysis and risk underwriting process to assign Obligors a Credit Risk rating or Credit Score that indicates the amount of Trade Debt that Obligor is likely to be able pay within certain Credit Periods. For example, based on its credit analysis, a TC Insurer may assign an Obligor a Credit Risk Rating or Score of 5 on its rating scale of 1 to 10. Under this hypothetical rating system, a rating of 5 might mean the Obligor is likely to be able to pay a Trade Debt up to $200,000 within a 90-day Credit Period. An Obligor rating of 10 might mean the Obligor is likely to be able to pay a Trade Debt up to $5,000,000 within a 5-year Credit Period, whereas a rating of 1 might mean the Obligor is not likely to able to pay that same debt. Obligor Credit Risk ratings and Scores can be used by a TC Insurer to guide its underwriting decisions, or its ratings may also be sold to Sellers and other Financiers to enable them to make their own Credit Risk decisions about their potential Obligors. The main difference between a Credit *Rating* and a Credit *Score* is that a Credit Score is usually a number derived from a mathematical formula using objective underwriting inputs (e.g., debt payment histories, available credit lines, usage, etc.), rather than a subjective underwriting *Rating*. The other practical difference is that in many places, such as Europe and the United States, Credit Ratings may be issued only by regulated and qualified rating agencies, whereas the issuance of Credit Scores for businesses (unlike for individuals) is largely unregulated.

Single Obligor Risks vs. Diversified Obligor Risks

Most, if not all, TC Insurers prefer to insure diverse groups (five or more) of Obligors in order to spread their risks and to avoid the risk of large one-off losses. Nevertheless, TC Insurers will often agree to cover a single Obligor, or very small groups of up to five or so Obligors, when requested by a Financier that is making a loan to a single Obligor or is purchasing only a portion of a Seller's AR payable by only a small group of its Buyers. However, TC Insurers will generally avoid insuring Obligors that the prospective insured selects because they are its least creditworthy ones, while it attempts to leave uninsured the rest of its more creditworthy Obligors. This attempt by the prospective insured to select only its riskiest Obligors for insurance is referred to as "adverse selection" and is a red flag for TC Insurers.

Discretionary Credit Limits (DCLs)

Sellers and other Financiers that, in the opinion of the TC Insurer, have an active and competent in-house Buyer or Obligor credit management operation may be given a Discretionary Credit Limit (DCL) that gives it discretion to add Buyers or Obligors under its TCI Contract without having to obtain the TC Insurer's pre-approval. The DCL will state the minimum underwriting conditions that each Buyer or Obligor must satisfy as a condition to coverage, which may include positive payment histories, credit ratings, or other criteria. Alternatively, the TC Insurer may simply agree to a DCL based exclusively on the insured's existing Buyer or Obligor credit management procedures, which may be incorporated into the TCI Contract by Endorsement.

TCI Contracts with DCLs will typically also include a Deductible, the amount of which is often, but not necessarily, correlated to some degree with the DCL amount. For example, an insured Seller with a TCI Contract covering $10 mm of insured Trade Debt, with a $500,000 Deductible, may be granted a DCL of up $500,000, allowing it to add Buyers with Credit Limits up to $100,000 each.

Whole Turnover vs. Excess of Loss Contracts

TC Insurers may provide two types of Insurance Contracts, Whole Turnover or Excess of Loss (XOL). Some TC Insurers offer both types, while other focus on only one. For Whole Turnover, or "ground up," TCI Contracts, the TC Insurer analyzes and underwrites the Credit Risk for each Obligor that it agrees to insure and assigns it a Credit Limit indicating its maximum coverage amount. The decision to cover any Obligor is at the sole discretion of the TC Insurer unless it has agreed to give the insured a DCL. Obligors with very low creditworthiness will typically be excluded from coverage. Whole Turnover Contracts typically have Indemnity Rates of 80% to 95% and may have Deductibles from 5% to 10%. A Whole Turnover Contract, for example, might provide the following coverage:

- Sales covered: $40,000,000, insuring 100 Obligors/Buyers
- Credit Limits: 50 Buyers with Credit Limits of $1,000,000 each and 50 Buyers with limits of $500,000 each (total Credit Limits of $75,000,000)
- Insurer's Maximum Liability: $25,000,000
- Indemnity Rate: 90%
- Insured Co-Insurance: 10%
- Premium: Based on Sales of $40,000,000 = Premium Rate of 0.50% (50 basis points) of Sales ($40,000,000) = total premium $20,000.
- Fees: 15% of Premium (15% of $20,000) = $3,000

For XOL Contracts, the TC Insurer analyzes the Credit Risks for the largest Obligors, in terms of insurable amounts, for which there should be readily available credit and underwriting data. XOL Contracts will include a relatively large first-loss Deductible and relatively large Discretionary Credit Limits. The relatively large Deductible may result in the insured sustaining a large amount of losses before the TC Insurer pays any claims. XOL Contracts are generally used to cover excessive, unexpected, or catastrophic losses.

Underwriting Large Portfolios of Obligors

TC Insurers that offer Whole Turnover Contracts are typically requested to insure all, or a majority, of a Seller's Obligors, which can easily number 100 or much more. The largest TC Insurers will receive numerous requests for insurance quotes each day, for which they are expected to conduct their underwriting and respond with a quote within 3 to 5 business days. In these cases, for the sake of time and efficiency, TC Insurers will typically analyze and underwrite only the Seller's ten or so largest Obligors in terms of Credit Limit amounts in order to produce a quote that will give the insured a good idea of the scope of coverage it is likely to receive on the rest of its Obligors. This preliminary quote will specify each analyzed Obligor's Credit Limit and the insured's price (premium and fees).

The number of analyzed and approved Obligors during this preliminary underwriting process in relation to those Obligors it declines to insure is called the TC

Insurer's "Acceptance Rate," which the prospective insured will use to decide whether to proceed and execute a TCI Contract, with an expectation that it will thereafter submit additional Obligors for underwriting decisions that result with the same or better Acceptance Rate. Acceptance Rates of approximately 75% to 80% are generally considered to be competitive. Lower Acceptance Rates, however, may be competitive for higher risk portfolios.

This process of underwriting a sampling of a prospective insured's top ten Obligors will work for insureds that are Sellers that can afford to submit the rest of their Obligors for underwriting over time. However, this sampling approach will not work for some Sellers, and especially not for Financiers that intend to purchase a predetermined portfolio of AR. These prospective insureds often require a full underwriting of each Obligor to be certain of each one's insurable Credit Limit, and its maximum possible insurance costs. In these cases, TC Insurers will try to limit this type of 100% Obligor underwriting process to opportunities that present the most potential income or client relationship gains.

Brokers

TCI Brokers are professional TCI specialists that represent and advise insureds in order to achieve for them the best possible coverage and terms. Brokers also function as a critical distribution and sales channel for TC Insurers. At an insured's request, a Broker will solicit quotes from one or more TC Insurers that they believe will provide the most competitive and timely quotes. A sufficient number of quotes should provide the insured with an accurate view of what the TCI market can offer. Brokers also advise insureds about which TC Insurer they should select based on offered Credit Limits, TCI Contract wording, customer service and experience, and claims reliability. A Broker may also provide assistance with claims filing and TCI Contract negotiation and management. Despite the fact that Brokers represent the insureds, Brokers earn commissions from the TC Insurer at rates that are generally between 15% to 20% of the paid premium amount. Brokers in most countries, or their political subdivisions, are subject to regulation and licensing. For example, in the United States, a Broker must be licensed by the State from which the Broker operates and the State from which the TCI Contract that it sells is issued. As licensed and regulated professionals, Brokers are responsible for any of their errors or omissions that harm their insureds (e.g., late claims filing, misleading or incorrect policy interpretations, etc.).

Insureds could approach TC Insurers directly for quotes without using a Broker. However, to be successful in doing so, the insured needs to have a good deal of expertise, experience, and up-to-date market information to know the most appropriate TC Insurers from which to seek quotes and to know how to effectively negotiate pricing and other terms. Additionally, there are hundreds of different coverages which most insureds are likely not aware of but which could make a great deal of difference to their coverage needs. Experienced Brokers specializing in TCI normally have this required level of expertise, and there is no cost savings in going it alone without a Broker because TC Insurers rarely, if ever, pass on commission savings to the insureds that do not use Brokers.

Agents

Agents typically represent one or more TC Insurers as their sales force, selling TCI directly to insureds or their Brokers. Agents may be either employees of a TC Insurer or independent contractors. In the United States, an Agent must be licensed by the State from which it operates and the State from which the TCI Contract they sell is issued. As licensed and regulated professionals, Agents are responsible for their errors or omissions that harm their insureds or the TC Insurer (e.g., late claims filing, misleading or incorrect policy interpretations, etc.).

TC Economics

When procuring and using TCI, it is useful to understand how TC Insurers operate and what drives their business and their underwriting and claims decision-making processes. Contrary to some popular misconceptions, TC Insurers really do pay legitimate claims. In some countries, such as the United States, they report their cost of paying claims on their balance sheet and to their regulators, so it is relatively easy to determine and prove how much a TCI Insurer actually pays in claims. A TC Insurer's annual cost of claims for all its insureds in relation to its earned annual premium for all its insureds is referred to as its annual "loss ratio." Loss ratios are also calculated for each of its insureds based on the TC Insurer's annual claim payments and premium history for that insured. Loss ratios are key measurements and strong indicators of a TC Insurer's financial health and underwriting competency, and the market conditions in which it is operating. To determine its "aggregate loss ratio" for any given accounting year, a TC Insurer takes into account claims paid in that particular accounting year plus claims paid under *loss attaching* policies in subsequent years for losses that arose during the original accounting year. For example, a TC Insurer's aggregate loss ratio for 2020 should include claims it paid in 2020, plus claims it paid in 2021 and subsequent years for losses that arose in 2020 under its *loss attaching* policies. Insurers will also measure current-year loss ratios that take into account only current-year claim payments in order to measure their current underwriting performance. An Insurer may have an acceptable aggregate loss ratio of 40%, but an unacceptable current loss ratio of 60%, which indicates either current-year underwriting problems, deteriorating market conditions, or some other cause that needs attention.

A key indicator of a TC Insurer's economic health and profitability is its annual Total Cost Ratio, which is a combination of its current-year loss ratio and its current-year operating cost ratio (its annual operating costs in relation to its annual revenue). For example, a TC Insurer with a current-year loss ratio of 40% and an operating cost ratio of 40% has a Total Cost Ratio of 80%, which should deliver the TC Insurer a net return of 20% in relation to its annual revenue. Generally, a TC Insurer's loss and cost ratios should each be below 50%, preferably between 30%

and 40%. Another key indicator of a TC Insurer's economic health is the annual rate at which it renews and retains existing profitable TCI Contracts. A healthy annual renewal rate should run 90% or higher under normal market conditions. Another key economic growth indicator is the annual rate at which the TC Insurer adds new Insurance Contracts and premiums, with a healthy range being from 5% to 15%.

Determining TCI Contract's Profitability – Loss Ratios

Profitable TCI Contracts are typically those in which the average aggregate annual loss ratios over three years or more are 45% or below, depending on the TC Insurer's average annual operating cost ratio for those years. In the United States, TCI Contracts can be cancelled only if the insured fails to pay owed premium. However, throughout the TCI Contract period, unless the TC Insurer has agreed to non-cancellable limits, it may reduce or cancel individual Buyer or Obligor Credit Limits when it perceives changes in its covered risks. A TC Insurer may also use its annual TCI Contract renewal negotiations to adjust terms when necessary to return the TCI Contract to profitability or to cancel it. These adjustments may include increasing the premium or fees, adding or increasing a Deductible, or reducing certain Buyer or Obligor Credit Limits. Conversely, if the insured believes its TCI Contract is priced is too high relative to its claims history, the insured may decide to negotiate more favorable terms with the TC Insurer during the renewal period. Renewal negotiations should typically begin 90 to 30 days prior to a TCI Contract's expiry date to give the parties time to evaluate their needs. Some TCI Contracts, however, will state that they will automatically renew annually unless one of the parties wants to make changes.

Insurance Regulation

TC Insurers, Brokers, and Agents are regulated by insurance or financial regulators and by applicable laws (anti-money laundering, business contracts, sanctions, etc.) in the countries in which they do business. In the United States, for example, each of the 50 States and the District of Columbia (D.C.), regulate TCI offered to insureds in their State (or in D.C.). TCI regulations govern the types of coverage and terms that may be offered, the TCI Contract's wording, the range of pricing and how it may be calculated, and the TC Insurer's economic viability to be able to pay claims. Regulators have the power to impose penalties, fines, and license revocations to enforce their rules. There is a fair amount of confusion and debate within the TC Industry as to the interpretation of some fundamental rules regarding where, how, and by whom TCI may be offered in places in which it has no permanent business operations. This debate is especially important, for example, regarding the extent to which a TC Insurer can provide insurance for an insured's business in a country in which the TC Insurer is not licensed to do business. For example, may a TC Insurer licensed only in the United States insure debts arising from a US business's Mexican subsidiary? Many countries have laws prohibiting foreign TC Insurers from providing insurance services within their country in order to protect both their native TC Insurers and insureds. To address this issue, a TC Insurer may take either a highly restrictive approach in which it will provide no or very little coverage for insureds in countries in which the TC Insurer is not licensed, or it may take a case-by-case approach based on its view of each foreign country's laws or its perceived risk of being penalized.

Claims

Broker acting on its behalf, will file claims for losses with its TC Insurer in accordance with the terms, procedures, and timing stated in its TCI Contract. If a Broker is involved, it should assist the insured with the claims submission. Common reasons TC Insurers deny claims include claims filed after their filing deadline, losses in excess of coverage limits, claims on incorrectly named Buyer or Obligor legal entities, excluded losses for deliveries to past due Buyers, and non-disclosure of adverse information to the TC Insurer.

Claims Adjustment

TC Insurers will adjust an insured's claim by evaluating its validity and the scope of applicable coverage and then deciding on the amount of the claim payment. Claims Adjustment is typically done by a TC Insurer's internal claims division or by a third-party operating on the TC Insurer's behalf.

Claims Waiting Period

The TCI Contract will state the number of days, typically 180 days or less, the insured must wait before for its claim will paid. A Waiting Period is imposed to give the insured time to use its best efforts to recover the loss through negotiations or other means. Insureds, therefore, need to take into account waiting periods when negotiating TF transactions to account for their cash flow, funding, and accounting needs.

POLITICAL RISK INSURANCE (PRI)

Political Risk Insurance (PRI) may be provided by governments, state-owned enterprises, or private insurers to one or more parties to a TF transaction, covering nonpayment of Trade Debt due to losses caused by a covered Political Risk. The US Export-Import Bank, for example, provides PRI to support US exports. PRI can also cover losses arising from non-TF transactions, including equity investment protections, loan defaults, asset expropriation, and other enterprise disruption risks. PRI-covered parties may include Sellers, Buyers, Obligors, Financiers, investors, or other parties with an economic interest at risk of loss due to Political Risks. Covered Political Risks may include actions taken by governmental bodies, their agencies, and government-owned enterprises, and events involving government actions (e.g., war, civil unrest). Covered Political Risks may include government actions that are general in their application (e.g., foreign currency transfer restrictions) or targeted directly at a specific transaction or party in a discriminatory manner (asset confiscation, license revocation).

Each PRI Insurer's coverage will vary depending on its capacity for certain risks and its business objectives. For example, some government Agencies, such as the US government's US International Development Finance Corporation (DFC), provide PRI to support US foreign policy interests through investments and transactions that are sponsored by, or involve in some way, US businesses.

Buyers, Sellers, Obligors, or Financiers to a TF transaction may purchase PRI against the risk of loss caused by the following most common Political Risks:

- war or civil unrest
- restrictions on the movement of funds or currency conversions
- trade embargoes or similar restrictions
- revocation of import, export, or other business licenses
- discriminatory taxation or levies
- contract frustration or breach
- government failures to enforce legal obligations, including court judgements, or arbitral awards
- Trade Debt payment default (e.g., AR or loan) by a government Buyer or Obligor
- government actions that prevent access to business premises, or expropriates funds, collateral, or other assets

Trade Debt Payment Default

PRI can insure a Financier against losses caused by a government or a government-owned enterprise, Buyer, Borrower or Guarantor failing to repay a Trade Debt. This type of cover is sometimes referred to as "Breach of Contract," referring to a Trade Debt agreement that is the breached contract, or "Non-Honoring of a Sovereign Guarantee" in cases in which a country refuses to honor its payment Guarantee of a Trade Debt. For example, a Financier makes a 5-year, $100 mm loan to a foreign state-owned oil company, the Buyer, to enable it to import drilling equipment from the Financier's client, the Seller. The Buyer's country issues a loan repayment Guarantee on behalf of the Buyer through the country's Ministry of Finance. A PRI Insurer issues the Financier a PRI Contract covering "Non-payment of a Sovereign Guarantee" in which the PRI Insurer agrees to pay the Financier up to 90% ($90 mm) of the loan amount in case of the Buyer's and its Guarantor's nonpayment. The PRI Insurer will agree to pay claims based on the original loan repayment schedule as each principal installment goes unpaid, or the PRI Insurer may agree to pay the insured in a lump sum if it believes the Buyer and Guarantor are likely to never honor all or part of the Trade Debt or the Guarantee. As is the case for most, if not all, TCI and PRI Contracts, premiums are calculated and due for the entire duration of the coverage period. In other words, a Financier procuring PRI coverage for a 5-year loan will owe the entire amount of premium to the PRI Insurer, whether the loan goes into default in year 1, year 5, or never. This premium obligation needs to be taken into account when structuring the Trade Debt and PRI to determine whether to add the total premium due to the principal of the Trade Debt and have it covered by PRI and repaid over time; or whether to require the Buyer to pay the premium up front as a condition to making the loan.

Arbitral Award Coverage

An insured, usually a Seller or Financier, may procure PRI to protect it against losses caused by a government's or a government-owned enterprise's failure to honor or enforce an arbitral award in favor of the insured for that government entity's failure to honor its Trade Debt or other contractual obligations to the insured. This type of cover is generally intended to cover contractual obligations where performance (e.g., construction, project completion) is a critical issue and for which arbitration is the most suitable means for dispute resolution. However, it may also be used to cover Trade Debt payment obligations as well. For example, a Financier makes a 12-year, $100 mm loan to a state-owned hospital in a foreign country to enable it to import medical equipment from the Financier's client, the Seller. The Buyer's country, usually through its Ministry of Finance, provides the insured with a loan repayment Guarantee. A PRI Insurer provides the insured Financier a PRI Contract covering it for up to 90% ($90 mm) of the Trade Debt amount, agreeing to pay claims if all three of the following conditions are satisfied: (a) the Trade Debt goes unpaid by the Buyer and the Guarantor; (b) the insured wins an arbitral award against the Buyer and Guarantor for the unpaid Trade Debt; and (c) the Buyer and Guarantor fail to honor the arbitral award decision.

Contract Frustration

Insureds can procure PRI to protect against the their risk of financial harm due to a government's or a government-owned enterprise's failure to honor its contractual obligations to the insured. Insurable contractual obligations may include Trade Debt repayment obligations; obligations to purchase Items; obligations to operate, fund or supply Items to a business upon which the insured is relying on for repayment of its Trade Debt; or other government obligations that must be honored for the successful execution of the insured transaction. For example, a Seller exports $30 mm of solar power equipment to a privately owned Buyer in foreign country, giving it 3 years to pay. The Ministry of Energy in the Buyer's country agrees to purchase solar power from that Buyer at rates that allow the Buyer to repay the Seller within 3 years and agrees to designate that Seller as a Beneficiary to that solar power purchase contract or agrees to let the Buyer assign its rights to the power purchase contract to the Seller. The Seller procures PRI that protects it against the risks of the Ministry of Energy failing to honor its power purchase contract with the Buyer. If the Buyer and the Ministry of Energy fail to pay the Seller, the PRI Insurer will pay the Seller the payment shortfall up to its agreed indemnity level (e.g., 90%) of the $30 mm export contract amount.

Export, Import, or Other Business License Revocation

Insureds may procure PRI to protect against losses caused by a country revoking the Seller's or Buyer's import, export, or other business license needed to execute its TF transaction. This coverage is useful to protect a Seller's pre-delivery costs used to produce finished goods that go unsold, or are sold for a lesser price to another Buyer, due to license revocation that causes the original Buyer's inability to honor its purchase obligations. For example, a Seller secures a contract to sell a country $10 mm of armored vehicles, which take the Seller one year to produce and deliver. The Seller procures PRI covering its production costs or its sales price against the risk that either the Seller's or Buyer's country revokes the export or import license and the Seller is unable to resell the vehicles to another party to mitigate all or part of its loss.

Currency Inconvertibility and Transfer Risk

PRI can protect an insured against losses caused by a country initiating new currency exchange and transfer restrictions that prevent the insured being paid for its Trade or Trade Debt. For example, a Seller exports food to its Buyer in another country and is entitled to payment in the amount of $1 mm. Given the Buyer's country's history of imposing currency restrictions, the Seller procures PRI to protect it against losses caused by inconvertibility and transfer risks imposed the Buyer's country. After the Seller delivers its Items to the Buyer, the Buyer's country imposes currency and transfer restrictions that prevent the Buyer from converting its local currency into US Dollars or transferring US Dollars abroad. The PR Insurer will pay the Seller's claim at the agreed Indemnity Rate (e.g., 90% = $900,000) on the condition that the Seller can demonstrate the change in currency and transferability laws caused the Buyer to be unable to pay, which usually requires evidence that the Buyer made a deposit of its local or hard currency in a bank in the Buyer's country in an attempt to make its payments to the Seller.

War and Civil Unrest

PRI can protect an insured against losses caused by war or civil unrest that prevents one or more parties to its TF transaction from fulfilling their obligations to the insured. For example, a Seller exports $10 mm of machines to a Buyer in another country that is not at war. The Buyer's country is in a politically volatile region, so the Seller procures PRI covering it against the risks of war and civil unrest in the Buyer's country. By the time the Seller's machines arrive in the Buyer's country, civil war or war with another country has broken out, resulting in the Seller's goods being stolen, confiscated, or damaged with no hope of recovery. Before paying a claim to the Seller for its losses, the PRI Insurer will require the Seller to demonstrate it has satisfied all the PRI Contract conditions, including taking any possible actions to mitigate its losses. For example, the insured should demonstrate that it either tried, or had no reasonable opportunity, to divert the delivery of machines prior to its arrival in the Buyer's country. If the PRI Contract conditions are satisfied, the PRI Insurer will pay the Seller's claim for the lost Items up the agreed indemnity amount (e.g., 90% of their sales price).

Confiscation or Expropriation

PRI can protect an insured against losses caused by government confiscating or expropriating its insured assets. For example, a Seller exports $50 mm of mining drills to a Buyer in another country, granting it Credit Terms allowing it 5 years to pay, on the condition that the Buyer creates and funds a Trade Debt service reserve account into which a share of its mining revenues will be deposited to create collateral to help secure repayment of its Trade Debt to the Seller. The Seller procures PRI covering the risks of the Buyer's country seizing or otherwise blocking access to the funds in the debt reserve account (the insured's collateral). If the Buyer's country confiscates the collateral and the Buyer is unable to pay the Seller from its other funds, the PRI Insurer will pay the Seller a claim for its unpaid amounts up to the agreed indemnity level.

Other Government Actions

PRI can cover other risks not described here that prevent one or more parties to a TF transaction from honoring their payment, delivery, or other obligations to the insured, based on the willingness and risk capacity of PR Insurers. Brokers specialized in PRI should be well positioned to find the appropriate PRI Insurer to cover such risks.

PRI Policy Exclusions

PRI Contracts commonly exclude coverage in cases where the insured or anyone acting on its behalf, including any local agents, engaged in corrupt or fraudulent acts to facilitate the insured TF transaction.

TRADE DEBT DISTRIBUTION

Trade Debt Distribution is a form of risk mitigation in which a Financier sells all or part of a Trade Debt to other Financiers by means of Assignment, Participations, or Endorsement. This form of risk mitigation through risk sharing allows Financiers to leverage their risk and balance sheet capacities in order to maximize the amount of TF they can provide. A Financier's ability to distribute its Trade Debt can be an essential key to it being able to provide optimum TF solutions to the widest group of clients. If a Financier can offer only TF that it can hold on its books to maturity, it will be very limited in terms of the amount and type of TF it can offer.

The manner and form used to distribute Trade Debt will depend on its structure, complexity, and whether it is documented in a manner that makes it freely and easily transferrable. For example, a negotiable Bill of Exchange is designed to be easily distributed among Financiers by having its Obligor's payment obligation stated clearly on a single document that can be transferred simply by Endorsement. Loans or AR Purchase Finance transactions, on the other hand, can be more complicated to distribute, requiring the parties to which the Trade Debt is to be distributed to engage in a detailed review and understanding, and sometimes renegotiation, of the original or proposed transaction documents as well as the negotiation of the asset distribution agreement.

Endorsement

The most common means by which Negotiable Trade Debt Instruments are sold from one Financier to another is by Endorsement. This requires the owner of the negotiable Trade Debt to sign ("endorse") the instrument to its subsequent Holder in Due Course. Any Holder in Due Course may enforce the Negotiable Instrument against the Issuer directly without involving any previous Holder.

Assignment

A Financier may sell all or part of its ownership interest in a Trade Debt by Assignment, whereby it transfers all of its contractual and legal rights, risks, rewards, and responsibilities, in relation to the Obligor, to the Financier buying its Trade Debt. An assignee "steps in the shoes" of the original Financier for its share of the Trade Debt. This means an assignee will receive the same rate of interest on the loan as the original Financier and can enforce and take legal actions directly against the Obligor in case of disputes, without the permission or cooperation of the original Financier. For example, a Financier creates a $100 mm loan and agrees to sell/assign 50% ($50 mm) of it to another Financier in exchange for $50 mm. The Financier to which 50% of the loan is assigned now has the same exact legal standing as the original Financier has in relation to the Obligor for its $50 mm share. In this example, the original Financier sold 50% of its loan "at par" for $50 mm based on the loan's original $100 mm valuation. However, if the loan's original market value had increased over time due to improving market pricing for its Obligor, the original Financier could sell 50% of its loan "at a premium," and thus charge more than $50 mm (e.g., $55 mm) for a 50% share. Conversely, if the loan's original market value decreased over time, the original Financier would have to sell a 50% share its loan "at a discount" for less than $50 mm (e.g., $45 mm).

Participation

A Financier can transfer all or part of its Trade Debt to one or more other Financiers by Participation. With a Participation, a Participant simply participates in the gains or losses of a transaction and is entitled to collect its agreed share of interest and fees to the extent the original Financier is able to collect them. Participants may also agree to receive less remuneration (e.g., smaller interest rate) than the original Financier. Importantly, a Participant does not enjoy the same contractual or legal rights or responsibilities in relation to the Obligor as the original Financier does and thus does not "step in the shoes" of the original Financier. Accordingly,

Participants must rely on the original Financier to enforce the Trade Debt against the original Obligor in case of any disputes.[5]

Participations are often used in transactions wherein Assignments or other overt asset transfers are prohibited in the original Trade Debt agreements, or when using an Assignment will be too difficult, too costly, or require new negotiations or transaction amendments, or when the original Financier chooses not to disclose to its client that it is selling all or part of its Trade Debt. For example, a Financier initiates a $100 million TF loan transaction and agrees to transfer by means of a Participation 50% ($50 million) of the loan to another Financier. The Obligor, which will likely not know that a portion of its Trade Debt was transferred to a Participant, will make its Trade Debt payments directly to the original Financier. That original Financier, will in turn, pass on to the Participant its share of the payments on the terms agreed in its Participation Agreement. Participations may also be done on an "unfunded" risk basis, in which the Participant delivers its share of funds only if the Obligor fails to honor its Trade Debt payment obligations. Unfunded risk Participations are, therefore, more like payment guarantees rather than actual funded asset transfers.

Forfaiting

Forfaiting is another form of Trade Debt Distribution, traditionally used in Europe, to describe a process by which banks would arrange short- and medium-term TF for Buyers using Negotiable Promissory Notes or Bills of Exchange instead of complex credit agreements in order to make the Trade Debt easily transferrable to the widest possible group of potential Financiers. With Forfaiting, a Trade Debt is sold ("forfeited"), typically by means of Endorsement, to other Financiers. The practice and the use of the term Forfaiting is generally limited to niche TF providers and is often specific to certain industries. The term Forfaiting is also used by some, mostly in Europe, to describe AR Purchase Finance. It may be interest bearing or simply an obligation to pay only a principal amount. A Forfaited Trade Debt that is to be paid in a series of principal payments, may be structured into a series of separate Negotiable Instruments, each representing a distinct maturity (e.g., a 90-day Draft, a 180-day Draft, and a 360-day Draft). Each Draft in the series may be sold to a single Financier or to different ones. In order for a Financier to earn a sufficient rate of interest, it will buy the Forfaited Trade Debt either (a) if it bears interest, at "*par*," being the principal amount payable by the Obligor as stated on the Trade Debt Instrument; (b) at a *discount,* being an amount less than par; or (c) at a *premium,* being an amount higher than par.

---

5   A Participant Financier may, however, exercise other legal rights as a Beneficiary to the transaction, depending on the legal regime in the country in which the parties may pursue legal remedies.

Syndication

Syndication is a distribution process in which a Financier organizes a group (a syndicate) of Financiers to share portions of a Trade Debt as co-Financiers. The Financier that arranges the transaction and organizes its syndication will typically earn a greater share of any fees to compensate it for these services. For example, a Financier initiates a TF loan that requires $150 million of funded risk and that Financier distributes one third of the transaction ($50 million each) to two other Financiers, each of which becomes a co-Lender on the loan. Syndications typically require the other Financiers to fund their respective share of a Trade Debt on its funding dates to avoid having any of the other Financiers temporarily bear the entire funding obligation on their own. Each syndication Financier is responsible to fund its share of the transaction on a timely basis, which means the lead Financier will select each potential syndicate member based on its creditworthiness and ability to fund and operate efficiently.

THIRD-PARTY PAYMENT GUARANTEES

Payment Guarantees are unconditional guarantees for payment, issued on behalf of a Buyer or Obligor, typically by its affiliate or parent company or a state-owned enterprise, in which the guaranteeing party (Guarantor) promises to pay a Seller or other Financier the Buyer's or Obligor's Trade Debt obligations.[6] The use of third-party guarantees is not the norm in TF and is considered an exceptional measure when the Buyer's or Obligor's creditworthiness is unknown or unacceptable. Governments may provide payment guarantees through their Export Credit Agencies (ECAs) for transactions that promote some policy interest, such as export or foreign investment promotion. Payment Guarantees can also take the form of irrevocable Standby Letters of Credit issued by a bank acting on behalf of the LC Applicant, usually a Buyer or Obligor, in which the LC bank guarantees the LC Applicant's payment obligation to the LC Beneficiary, usually the Seller or other Financier. Banks in the US and in some other countries are not allowed to provide financial guarantees unless they are in the form of a Standby Letter of Credit.

The substance of any unconditional payment Guarantee, in whatever form it takes, should state at a minimum that it is an absolute, unconditional Guarantee of payment, and not merely collection, and that it is payable on demand (i.e., no waiting periods), and that the Guarantor waives any defense to payment. The express terms of the Guarantee should make clear that the guaranteed party should not have to prove anything to the Guarantor or to a Standby LC Bank other than the fact it did not receive the guaranteed payment by the due date.

---

6 Parent and holding companies, unless they issue an unconditional payment Guarantee, are generally not legally responsible for their subsidiary's or affiliate's financial obligations, even though they often claim they will nevertheless likely "support" them in the event of their bankruptcy. History, however, has shown that this "support" can disappear when it makes economic sense for the parent or holding company.

DOCUMENTARY LETTER OF CREDIT (DOC-LC)

A Documentary Letter of Credit (Doc-LC) is a bank-intermediated payment instrument used by Buyers and Sellers to ensure that a Seller is paid what it is owed after it delivers Items to its Buyer according to the terms of their Trade agreement. Doc-LCs have been used for over 100 years using the assistance of trusted bank intermediaries as a means to facilitate trade among parties that do not trust each other to honor their delivery or payment obligations.[7] Buyers and Sellers that are concerned about these risks will condition the validity of their Trade agreement on the issuance of an acceptable Doc-LC. The future of Doc-LCs, however, is uncertain due to the evolution of modern trade practices, improved communications, and the availability of better credit and performance information, all of which has resulted in more cost-effective solutions than Doc-LCs to address delivery and payment risks among trading partners.[8] Nevertheless, Doc-LCs are still used in cross-border Trades (Imports and Exports).

The Uniform Customs and Practices for Documentary Credits (UCP), published by the International Chamber of Commerce (ICC), provides internationally accepted rules for Doc-LCs, the most recent revisions of which, at the time of this writing, were issued in 2007 and are referred to as the UCP 600. Nearly all Doc-LCs used for TF will state that the Doc-LC is subject to the UCP, referencing the most up-to-date revisions in effect at the time of the Doc-LC's Issuance and noting any UCP articles that do not apply or are amended for that specific Doc-LC. Doc-LCs that expressly incorporate the UCP rules make the rules legally binding on the parties as a contractual matter. Doc-LCs should also state which country's or other legal authority's (e.g., US States) laws will govern it and in which courts or forums legal disputes may be adjudicated.

The eUCP is a supplement to the UCP and is for use with LCs involved in e-Commerce and the exchange and negotiation of digital LC documentation. The eUCP, among other things, allows for electronic presentation of LC required documents and records (e.g., in PDF format) and electronic signatures and the use of the internet or other agreed means of electronic transmission.

---

7   Letters of credit are estimated to cover 12.5% of world trade, or $2.3 trillion, while documentary collections cover 1.7% of world trade, or $310 billion). See Friederike Niepmann and Tim Schmidt-Eisenlohr, "Trade Finance Around the World", VoxEU, June 11, 2016, https://voxeu.org/article/trade-finance-around-world

8   GTR – Global Trade Review reports that "The general long-term market trend is moving away from letters of credit as, up until the recent financial crisis, importers and exporters were becoming more confident in trading with each other on an open account basis. Companies became more than happy to take on certain risks and deal with certain countries. What's more, the trade credit insurance market has been growing. Some trade transactions are conducted with just insurance providing a way of mitigating nonpayment risks. https://www.gtreview.com/letter-of-credit.

How Doc-LCs Work

A Buyer, acting as the LC Applicant, will request a bank, acting as the LC Issuing Bank, with which it has a credit line, to issue its irrevocable promise to pay the Seller, acting as the LC Beneficiary, the amounts the Seller is owed by the Buyer once the Items are delivered according the parties' Trade agreement. The Seller will be paid, either at the offices of the LC Issuing Bank or at another bank authorized or nominated by the LC Issuing Bank.

The LC Issuing Bank or the LC Beneficiary may designate an LC Advising Bank, typically located in the LC Beneficiary's city or country, to deliver the Doc-LC to the Beneficiary and to authenticate it. Authentication can be made by several means, typically using some form of secure electronic communications. Apart from authenticating the Doc-LC and possibly transmitting the LC Beneficiary's documents to the LC Issuing Bank, the LC Advising Bank does not owe any other obligations to the LC Beneficiary nor guarantees it any of the Doc-LC parties' payment or other obligations.[9]

If the Seller does not know the LC Issuing Bank or trust it due to perceived credit, political, or other risks, the LC Beneficiary or the LC Issuing Bank can request a willing LC Confirming Bank to add its "confirmation" to the Doc-LC. The LC Confirming Bank can also authenticate the Doc-LC for itself and the LC Beneficiary. LC Confirming Banks will (a) receive, review, and approve the documents required for payment presented to it by the LC Beneficiary; and (b) pay the LC Beneficiary according to the terms agreed in the Doc-LC. An LC Confirming Bank substitutes its risk of payment for that of the LC Issuing Bank, creating a legal payment obligation to the LC Beneficiary equal to that of the LC Issuing Bank. Importantly, the LC Issuing Bank must expressly authorize the LC Confirming Bank to add its confirmation in order for the LC Confirming Bank, after it pays the LC Beneficiary upon presentation of conforming Doc-LC documents, to have a legal right to claim reimbursement from the LC Issuing Bank.[10]

If the LC Issuing Bank does not authorize the LC Confirming Bank, the LC Beneficiary may, nevertheless, contract with a bank of its choosing to add its unauthorized confirmation to the Doc-LC, thus creating a "silent" confirmation. However, the bank adding its silent, unauthorized confirmation to a Doc-LC will not benefit from the contractual reimbursement rights against the LC Issuing Bank that are enjoyed by authorized LC Confirming and LC Nominated Banks.[11]

---

9   Most LCs are transmitted and authenticated using a worldwide financial messaging network which exchanges messages between banks, initiated and operated by the Society of Worldwide Interbank Financial Telecommunication (SWIFT), that was formed in 1973 and is headquartered in Brussels. SWIFTNet is the infrastructure used to exchange these documents among 8740 financial institutions in 209 countries.

10   UCP 600 article 7.

11   UCP 600.

To receive payment, the LC Beneficiary presents to an LC Negotiating Bank the documents specified in the Doc-LC to prove that the correct Items have been delivered in accordance with the Buyer's and Seller's Trade agreement. The LC Negotiating Bank's role is to review the LC Beneficiary's documents and to verify whether they conform to the Doc-LC's requirements. Any documents presented by the LC Beneficiary that do not conform to the Doc-LC requirements will be deemed discrepant by the LC Negotiating Bank and will be rejected, unless the LC Applicant agrees to accept them or the discrepant documents are corrected and resubmitted by the LC Beneficiary. Common discrepancies can include Item delivery dates that fall outside the time periods allowed in the Doc-LC or incorrect or incomplete Item descriptions or quantities. The time, costs, and fees associated with transmitting and reviewing LC documents among the parties and managing discrepancies can create significant inefficiencies in the use of Doc-LCs. [12] The LC Beneficiary will also be required by the terms of the Doc-LC to present its Bill of Exchange, or Draft, that demands (as the Draft's Drawer) its payment from the LC Issuing Bank (the Draft's Drawee) or another Drawee bank stipulated in the Doc-LC. The Doc-LC will state that the LC Beneficiary is to be paid either (a) at "Sight" immediately upon presentation of conforming documents, after giving the reviewing bank a reasonable number of days for review them, making it a "Sight LC"; or (b) according to a deferred payment schedule stated in the Doc-LC, making it a "Deferred payment LC"; or (c) according to a deferred (e.g., 30, 60, 90 days) payment schedule stated in the LC Beneficiary's Bill of Exchange, now referred to as a "Time Draft," and thus making it a "Usance LC." Time Drafts should be accepted by the Issuing or Confirming Bank, making them payable by the accepting party and transferrable to other parties, as any other Negotiable Debt Instrument would be.

The Doc-LC will state whether it can be negotiated only by the LC Issuing Bank, a bank authorized by it, or by any bank selected by the LC Beneficiary. If the LC is freely negotiable at any bank, the Beneficiary may select its preferred bank, making it an Negotiating and Confirming Bank. The LC Issuing Bank may also choose to authorize the LC Nominated Bank to act on its behalf to review and negotiate conforming Doc-LC documents and to pay the LC Beneficiary. An authorized LC Nominated Bank thus performs the same functions as an LC Confirming Bank but with the key difference that an LC Nominated Bank does not substitute its payment risks for those of the LC Issuing Bank nor obligates itself to pay the LC Beneficiary in case the LC Issuing Bank fails to honor its payment obligations. If the LC Beneficiary presents conforming documents to the LC Nominated Bank and it pays the LC Beneficiary, the LC Issuing Bank is obligated to reimburse its LC Nominated Bank. [13]

---

12   The ICC's Publication 745 contains the International Standard Banking Practice for the Examination of Documents under Documentary Credits (ISBP), which is intended to provide guidance to a bank's LC document examiners for determining whether the Beneficiary's presented documents are compliant with the terms of the LC.

13   UCP 600 article 7. Under article 12 of UCP 600, "Unless a nominated bank is the confirming bank, an authorization to honor or negotiate does not impose any obligation on that nominated bank to honour or negotiate, except when expressly agreed to by that nominated bank and so communicated to the beneficiary."

Given the numerous rules and varying customs and practices surrounding Doc-LCs, structuring and executing them can become complicated and typically requires specialist teams within banks to administer them. The following describes how a basic Doc-LC operates:

1) Trade Agreement. The Buyer and Seller enter into a Trade agreement that is conditioned on the issuance of a Doc-LC by a bank acceptable to the Seller.

2) LC Application. The Buyer, as the LC Applicant, requests the issuance of a Doc-LC from a bank that is willing to provide it Credit Terms. Its application is usually made to a bank with which the Buyer has an existing LC credit line established. If not, the Buyer will need to shop around for a bank willing to issue the Doc-LC.

3) LC Reimbursement Agreement. The LC Applicant enters into an LC Reimbursement Agreement with the LC Issuing Bank, in which it agrees to reimburse the LC Issuing Bank for any LC disbursements it makes on its behalf, either at the time of each LC disbursement or within a number of days following disbursement (e.g., 30, 60, 90 days or more).

4) LC Issuance. The LC Issuing Bank issues the Doc-LC in favor of the LC Beneficiary (the Seller) and delivers it to the LC Beneficiary through an LC Advising Bank or LC Confirming Bank, or directly to the LC Beneficiary by courier or electronic means. The manner in which the LC Issuing Bank transmits the Doc-LC directly to LC Beneficiary depends on the LC Beneficiary's ability to authenticate the LC for itself. The LC will state the deadline (LC Expiry Date) by which time the LC Beneficiary must present to the LC Issuing Bank or other authorized Negotiating or Confirming Bank the documents listed in the LC (e.g., Invoices, transport documents, etc.). The LC also states whether the LC Beneficiary's negotiation and payment under the LC is restricted to the Issuing Bank.[14]

5) Items Delivered. The Seller delivers Items to the Buyer according to the terms of their Trade agreement. The parties may define delivery as providing services, making Items available for the Buyer to pick up at the Seller's place of business, the Seller delivering the Items at the Buyer's place of business, the Seller placing the Items on an ocean or other carrier, or any other agreed definition of delivery that makes it clear when and how legal title and ownership of the Items is transferred to the Buyer. The agreed delivery terms will also normally address which party is responsible for procuring insurance to cover damage or loss of the Items during delivery.

---

14 Until 1974, most letters of credit were communicated by mail, cable, or telex. Article 4 of the 1974 revision of the UCP reflected this practice by listing "cable, telegram or telex" as the means with which to "instruct" letters of credit. Boris Kozolchyk, "The Paperless Letter of Credit and Related Documents of Title," Law and Contemporary Problems 55(3), 39-101.

6) LC Document Presentation. The LC Beneficiary presents required documents by courier or by electronic means to the LC Issuing Bank in one or more presentations prior to LC Expiry Date, which should have been determined to afford the LC Beneficiary sufficient time to prepare and deliver the Items (e.g., 3 to 12 months).

7) Documents required for presentation commonly include negotiable or other permitted types of transport documents (bills of lading, truck or airway bills), which provide the document's Holder (the LC Applicant-Buyer) the right to take delivery of Items from the carrier at the place of delivery (port, airport, truck depot) by presenting or surrendering the original transport document to that carrier. Not all transport documents are freely negotiable to any Holder, and some may restrict the release of Items to only the parties named in the document.

8) Pro Forma Commercial Invoice, which is a pre-delivery billing statement issued by the Seller and addressed to the Buyer describing the Items (e.g., weights, measurements and quantities) and stating the amounts due for the Items at delivery, which may include taxes or other charges. It is used to prepare the Buyer for payment and to provide information required by shippers and tax, customs, or other authorities that may need the information as a condition to allowing the transaction or delivery to proceed.

9) Commercial Invoice issued by the Seller and addressed to the Buyer describing the Items and their price and weight, if applicable.

10) Certificate of Origin typically issued by a Chamber of Commerce in the country from which the Items originated.

11) Inspection Certificate issued by a public or private company certifying some quality or quantity aspect of the Items.

12) Insurance Certificate evidencing the Items are insured for losses during transport.

13) If Items are services, Work Performance or Completion Certificates evidencing delivery of satisfactory services, issued by a party agreed to in the parties' Trade agreement.

14) LC Beneficiary's Draft, a Bill of Exchange demanding immediate (i.e., at sight) or deferred payment from the LC Issuing Bank, or if the Seller had agreed to provide its Buyer with Credit Terms, its Bill of Exchange would be in the form of a Time Draft, which requires payment after a period of time (e.g., 30, 60, 90 days).

15) The LC Issuing Bank reviews the LC Beneficiary's documents to verify that they conform to the terms of the Doc-LC. If any documents fail to satisfy the terms of the LC, they are deemed discrepant, in which case the LC Issuing Bank may seek a waiver from LC Applicant or require corrected documents from the LC Beneficiary.

16) If the LC Issuing Bank or other authorized LC Negotiating or Confirming Bank verifies the LC Beneficiary's documents conform, it will pay the LC Beneficiary according to the terms of its Draft.

17) After making each payment, the LC Issuing Bank demands reimbursement from the LC Applicant in accordance with the parties' LC Reimbursement Agreement.

Doc-LC Costs

The types of typical LC costs summarized below, and which party pays them, are subject to negotiation and the customs and practice of the banks involved.

- LC Advising Bank fees are payable by the LC Beneficiary or the LC Issuing Bank to the LC Advising Bank and are typically a fixed dollar amount or a flat percentage rate calculated on the LC amount.

- LC Negotiation fees are generally payable by the LC Beneficiary to the LC Negotiating Bank as a flat percentage rate calculated on the LC amount being negotiated.

- Discrepancy fees are payable to the LC Negotiating Bank by the LC Beneficiary and are typically a fixed dollar amount per discrepancy.

- LC Confirmation fees are paid by the LC Beneficiary to the LC Confirming Bank. The fee is calculated as a per month, per quarter, or per annum percentage rate on the average daily amount available to be drawn under the LC and is based on the LC Issuing Bank's creditworthiness.

- The LC Applicant will pay the LC Issuing Bank an LC Issuance fee at a per annum percentage rate based on the LC Applicant's creditworthiness and calculated on the average daily amount available to be drawn under the LC.

- If the LC Applicant is provided additional time to reimburse the LC Issuing Bank after each LC disbursement (e.g., 30, 60, 90 days or more), the LC Applicant will pay the LC Issuing Bank interest calculated as a per annum percentage rate on the amounts disbursed under the LC, until they are paid by the LC Applicant, and based on the LC Applicant's creditworthiness.

Documentary Letter of Credit Contract

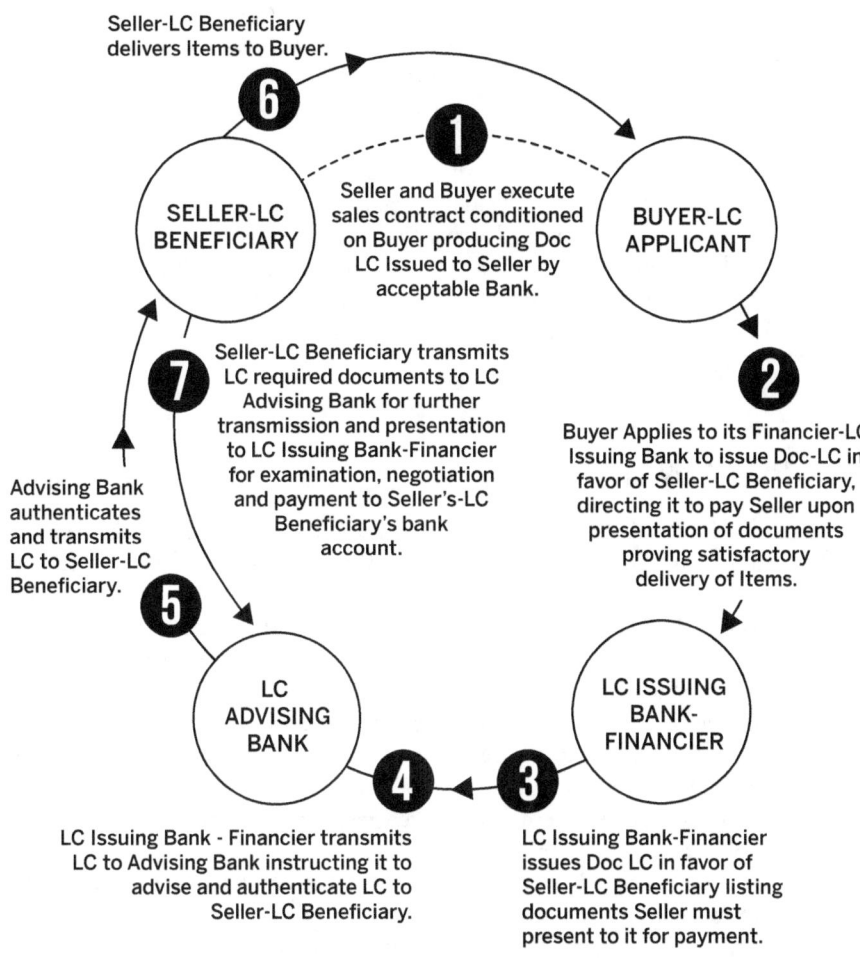

Seller-LC Beneficiary delivers Items to Buyer.

6

SELLER-LC BENEFICIARY

1 Seller and Buyer execute sales contract conditioned on Buyer producing Doc LC Issued to Seller by acceptable Bank.

BUYER-LC APPLICANT

2 Buyer Applies to its Financier-LC Issuing Bank to issue Doc-LC in favor of Seller-LC Beneficiary, directing it to pay Seller upon presentation of documents proving satisfactory delivery of Items.

7 Seller-LC Beneficiary transmits LC required documents to LC Advising Bank for further transmission and presentation to LC Issuing Bank-Financier for examination, negotiation and payment to Seller's-LC Beneficiary's bank account.

Advising Bank authenticates and transmits LC to Seller-LC Beneficiary.

5

LC ADVISING BANK

LC ISSUING BANK-FINANCIER

4 **3**

LC Issuing Bank - Financier transmits LC to Advising Bank instructing it to advise and authenticate LC to Seller-LC Beneficiary.

LC Issuing Bank-Financier issues Doc LC in favor of Seller-LC Beneficiary listing documents Seller must present to it for payment.

TCI OPTION: TCI may cover LC Issuing Bank against risk of Buyer-LC Applicant failing, due its financial inability, to reimburse for LC payments made to the LC Seller-Beneficiary.

STANDBY LETTERS OF CREDIT

Standby LCs, rather than an intermediated payment instrument such as a Doc-LC, may be used in TF transactions as a form of payment Guarantee in favor of a Seller or a Financier. Standby LCs may also be used to guarantee payments due from the Issuer of a Trade Debt, for example, issuers of loans, promissory notes, or Bills of Exchange. A Standby LC Issuing Bank, acting at the request and on behalf of the Standby LC Applicant (usually a Buyer), will issue a Standby LC in favor of the Standby LC Beneficiary (usually the Seller or Financier) stating its commitment to pay the LC Beneficiary in the event the LC Applicant fails to pay the amount agreed in the parties' Trade agreement. UCP 600 (Article 1) provides a set rules the parties to a Standby LC may incorporate by reference to their Trade agreement. The International Chamber of Commerce also publishes a different set of rules the parties can apply called the International Standard Practices 98 (ISP98). While both sets of rules are similar, most banks using Standby LCs apply the UCP 600 rules.

AGENCY FINANCE

National and international Agencies and institutions provide TF risk mitigation in the form of payment guarantees, TCI, and PRI, or provide TF directly in the form of loans or other forms of Trade Debt. Examples include national Export Credit Agencies, Development Banks, the World Bank, the International Finance Corporation (IFC), the Multilateral Guarantee Agency (MIGA), European Bank for Reconstruction and Development (EBRD), and KfW. Some of these Agencies also provide quasi-TF financing, such as Project or Commodity Finance, or asset-based working capital loans. Each national Agency's purpose or mission varies, but it is typically to promote and support that nation's foreign policy, trade, investment, or other goals. International Agencies' objectives are focused on global or regional objectives, most typically on reducing poverty and supporting economic and social development by providing TF, technical assistance, grants, or equity investments to enterprises in challenging credit markets. Many regional Agencies deliver the bulk of their TF financial assistance by guaranteeing trade-related bank-issued payment obligations, including LCs, Supply Chain Finance, and pre-shipment financing obligations, issued by participating banks. Below is a sampling of Agencies that provide some form of TF and other financial assistance. Details about their various TF and other financing solutions can best be explored through their respective websites, as a comprehensive description of each Agency's programs, products, and policies could easily fill a single book.

World Bank

Among the numerous multilateral and regional finance Agencies, the World Bank is the most active in the field of TF and provides the largest amount of multilateral development financing in the world. It provides loans, guarantees, risk management products, and advisory services to middle-income and creditworthy low-income countries. Its purpose is to provide financial assistance to end extreme poverty and to promote income growth among the world's poorer citizens. The World Bank's member Agency, MIGA, provides PRI and payment guarantees, some of which can be used as to support TF by managing and mitigating a Financier's repayment risks for TF or investment debt in which a sovereign or its subdivisions is a Borrower or Guarantor of payment or performance. Another World Bank member Agency, the IFC, acts as a Financier and financial advisor to promote economic development by supporting private sector investments in less developed countries by providing loans and other forms of debt and equity investments. The IFC also provides TF by guaranteeing trade-related bank-issued payment obligations (e.g., letters of credit) in challenging credit markets.

Asian Development Bank (ADB)

The Asian Development Bank's mission is to reduce poverty throughout Asia and the Pacific region by providing loans, credit guarantees, technical assistance, grants, and equity investments to support economic and social development. It provides TF by guaranteeing trade-related bank-issued payment obligations, including LCs, SCF, and pre-shipment financing obligations.

Banco Latinoamericano de Comercio Exterior, S.A. (BLADEX)

BLADEX is a multinational bank. Founded in 1977 as Banco Latinoamericano de Exportaciones, S.A. and renamed in June 2009, the company is headquartered in Panama City and finances Latin American and Caribbean foreign trade by offering a range of TF products and solutions for trade within or from its member countries.

Inter-American Development Bank (IDB)

The IDB supports economic and social development in Latin America and the Caribbean by providing financial assistance in the form of loans to government and state-owned business. Its member Agency, IDB Invest, provides TF through its participating banks.

KfW (Kreditanstalt für Wiederaufbau – Credit Institute for Reconstruction)

KfW is a German state-owned development bank. Its mission is to promote investments that support foreign trade from Germany and Europe and economic and social development globally. Its bank, KfW IPEX-Bank, provides a range of TF and quasi-TF to support transactions and projects sponsored by German or European businesses to help strengthen their respective export industries.

Brazil's National Bank for Economic and Social Development (BNDES)

BNDES is Brazil's development bank, whose mission is to provide TF, project finance, and other financial assistance to Brazilian businesses to promote exports, global expansions, and development, economic, and social development in Brazil.

United States International Development Finance Corporation (DFC)

The DFC is the United States's development bank. Its mission is to promote US foreign policy by supporting private sector investments and transactions in challenging credit markets. It provides financing assistance in the form of PRI, equity finance, loans, and technical advice.

Japan's Bank for International Cooperation (JBIC)

JBIC is Japan's development bank, whose mission is to promote and support Japanese economic policy and development by offering various forms of TF and other finance.

National Export Credit Agencies' (ECAs)

ECAs promote their respective country's exports by providing TF, which may include loans, payment guarantees, TCI, and PRI, to Sellers, Buyers, and Financiers to help their country's exporters compete effectively against foreign competition. ECAs are intended to be the Financiers of last resort in cases where the ECAs can offer Credit Terms that are not available in the private market and where there is foreign competition offering non-market Credit Terms.

To maintain a level playing field among competing ECAs, most countries offering Export Credits agree to a set of rules that govern and equalize the type and scope of Export Credit assistance that is allowed to be offered. The rules are administered through the Organisation for Economic Co-operation and Development's (OECD) nonbinding "Arrangement on Officially Supported Export Credits." Parties to the Arrangement, as of the time of this writing, are the USA, Australia, Canada, the European Union, Japan, Korea, New Zealand, Norway, Switzerland, and Turkey. The Arrangement applies to Export Credits with a Credit Period of two or more years, and regulates the maximum repayment terms, risk premium rates, interest rates, and other financing conditions. The Arrangement does not apply to exports of agricultural commodities or military equipment. Within the Arrangement are specific rules called Sector Understandings that regulate ECA assistance for certain industrial sectors, including (a) ships; (b) nuclear power plants; (c) civil aircraft; (d) renewable energy, climate change mitigation and adaptation, and water projects; (e) rail infrastructure; and (f) coal-fired electricity generation projects.

Examples of ECAs include the US Export-Import Bank (USA), Euler Hermes (Germany), Export Development Canada (EDC; Canada), Sinosure (China), Nippon Export and Investment Insurance (NEXI; Japan), Bpifrance Assurance Export (France), and Compañía Española de Seguros de Crédito a la Exportación (CESCE; Spain).

National Export Credit Programs

Operating within the parameters of the OECD Arrangement, each ECA's financial assistance program is unique to that country. For example, most ECAs provide loan repayment in the form of *insurance* that covers less than 100% (e.g., 90% to 95%) of an insured loan's principal and interest at risk. In contrast, the USA's ECA provides loan *guarantees* that cover 100% of the guaranteed loan's principal and interest. Some ECAs offer short-term TCI that is not covered by the Arrangement, while others leave this type of TCI to private TC Insurers. A summary of each ECA's programs is published, with varying degrees of clarity and details, on its respective website. Due to the scope and level of detail involved in each ECA's specific program, rules, policies, and processes, providing a comprehensive explanation of each of the 40 or more ECAs' programs would require an entire book for each one. Nevertheless, the key features common to the most active ECA programs are described below:

- ECAs provide support in the form of (a) direct loans to foreign Buyers importing Items from Seller's in the ECA's country; or (b) loan guarantees or insurance to Financiers that provide loans to those foreign Buyers; and (c) interest rate support in various forms to help equalize competition among ECAs.

- ECAs divide each Trade into two parts: (Part A) 85% of the Trade contract amount, for which the ECA may provide a direct loan or a payment Guarantee or insurance to a Part A Financier; and (Part B) the remaining 15% of the Trade contract amount, which is required to be either financed by the Seller or paid to the Seller in advance by the Buyer or by a Part B Financier. ECAs do not provide any financing support for Part B.

- For example, if the Trade contract = $100,000,000, Part A equals 85% ($85,000,000 plus interest and fees in some circumstances), for which an ECA may provide a loan, a payment Guarantee, or insurance. Part B is the remaining 15% ($15,000,000).

- ECAs must charge Buyers, or their Part A Financiers, approximately the same risk-based fees, typically called risk premiums or exposure fees, based on methodologies and risk ratings consistent with the Arrangement.

- Credit Periods and amortization schedules must conform to the type of exported Items, which are intended to correlate in length to the Items' average useful life. Export Credits normally begin amortizing no later than 6 months after the final Credit Advance, noting that it is common in export Trades for Items to be delivered over a period of one or more years.

- ECA Credit Periods normally fall into three categories: short-term (2 years or more); medium-term (3 to 6 years), and long-term (7 to 12 years), the latter of which applies to very large capital equipment expenditures, including those for rail cars, ships, and airplanes. For example, Credit Periods for certain capital equipment (e.g., heavy machinery, earth moving and farm equipment) are restricted to 5 to 7 years, while Credit Periods for large passenger jets are restricted to 12 years.

- ECA-supported finance may use variable or fixed interest rates, and several ECAs provide or subsidize fixed-rate loans.

- A minimum amount of national export content (e.g., 50% to 100%) of each Item is required to have been produced in the ECA's country.

- A certain maximum amount of foreign export content may be allowed (e.g., up to 15%) to be incorporated in the exported Items. These foreign content rules vary greatly by percentage and definition by each ECA.

Example - Basic Medium-Term Export Credit Using the US Export-Import Bank

Export of Farm Equipment (tractors) to a Buyer in Asia

US Export Contract Value	$100,000,000
Eligible Export Contract Amount (Part A - 85%)	$85,000,000
US EXIM's Exposure Fee (Risk Premium) (5% of $85,000,000)	$ 4,250,000
Export Credit Amount	$89,250,000
Export Credit Period:	5 and ½ years

Export Credit Amortization Period: 5 years, made in 10 equal, semi-annual principal payments, beginning 6 months after the final Credit Advance, which would be 6 months after the loan is executed.

Form of Export Credit: Either (a) a loan for $89,250,000, provided by US EXIM directly to the Buyer; or (b) a loan for $89,250,000, provided by a Financier to the Buyer, the repayment of which is guaranteed 100% by US EXIM.

Interest Rate: Either (a) a fixed interest rate based on US EXIM's interest rate program if the Export Credit is a loan provided by US EXIM; or (b) a floating or fixed interest rate if the loan is provided by the Buyer's Financier.

FRAUD RISK MITIGATION

The most effective way to mitigate or prevent fraud risk is to *know your client* (KYC) and its business, and by having well-trained employees to be sensitive and alert to recognizing red flags, and by maintaining business operations and practices designed to prevent or detect fraud. Meaningful KYC involves more than simply checking off boxes in a KYC review process designed to meet a regulator's minimum diligence standards. A good practice for every transaction party is to conduct its own due diligence to verify the identity, location, and financial condition of each transaction party. To detect potential TF fraud, diligent parties should make it a practice to be alert to the potential anti-fraud red flags published by their respective regulators, all of which well-informed but corrupt parties are also aware. Other red flags especially applicable to TF include the following:

- A Financier or other party is offered exceptional or non-market terms to induce light due diligence or KYC scrutiny and to "look the other way." For example, Sellers or Financiers may be offered above-market pricing to transact with parties about which it may have very little knowledge and whose minority or silent owners may be on a sanctions list.

- A party insists on working exclusively with a single person within a Financier's or other party's organization, with whom it may be scheming to commit fraud. This is one reason many Financiers maintain a "two eyes" principal, which requires that at least two people sign contracts, and for banks in the United States, a requirement that employees spend at least two weeks per annum away from the office without having any contact with their business, both of which rules make solo fraud more difficult.

- A transaction with one or more red flags (e.g., high-fraud-risk country or industry or unknown parties) may involve a presumably innocent and respected business or government institution such as an ECA in the transaction, which may be being used to give the transaction the cover of legitimacy. For example, fraudulent transactions may begin with an initiating party promising the future involvement of a well-known Financier or government payment Guarantee in order to induce the other parties to take the transaction seriously. Once the transaction gains momentum, the promised Guarantor either does not materialize or is replaced with an inferior Guarantor that helps carry out the fraudulent transaction.

CHAPTER 4

TF Structures, Solutions, and Products

Described below are the TF structures, solutions, and products most used globally and domestically, and how the various TF risk mitigation tools are used to facilitate them.

SELLER FINANCING

Seller financing is by far the most widely used form of TF globally. Unless a Seller demands cash from its Buyer at delivery, it will typically allow its Buyer 30, 60, or even, exceptionally, 90 days after delivery in which to pay for its Items. Delivery can mean physical delivery to the Buyer, or whatever delivery process the parties agree to in their Trade agreement. Each time a Seller grants its Buyer time to pay, it becomes the Buyer's Financier and creates an AR in its accounting books and records as an asset which remains an "open account" until it is paid. At the same time the AR is created, the Buyer creates and records a corresponding Trade Payable in its accounting books and records as a liability.

A condition for creating a valid and legally enforceable AR is the Seller having delivered Items in accordance with its Trade agreement with the Buyer. If the Buyer legitimately disputes the Trade on the grounds that the Items did not conform to the Trade agreement, then the Seller does not have valid legal claim for payment for the value of the nonconforming Items. It is common in the case of a Trade Dispute that if the Buyer intends to make more Trades with that Seller in the future, it may decide to accept and pay the full AR amount in exchange for receiving a credit from the Seller (sometimes referred to as a "credit memo") for the disputed amount which will be deducted from future purchases. Conforming Items that later prove faulty after the Buyer's AR payment are typically addressed by the Seller's warranty without diluting the value of the original AR.

The Buyer is normally not a party to any document promising to pay the AR unless the parties have entered into a written sales agreement that contains AR payment obligations, or a separate Trade Debt agreement. The parties may agree to document the Buyer's Trade Payable in the form of a Trade Debt, such as a negotiable Bill of Exchange or Promissory Note, in order to make it more easily transferrable to other Financiers. If the Seller decides to provide its Buyer with extended payment terms (e.g., 1 year or more), it will typically enter into a formal written Trade Debt agreement with the Buyer (e.g., loan, Promissory Note, or Bill of Exchange) in which the Buyer has effectively acknowledged receipt of conforming Items, thereby waiving any defenses to payment. Any disputes between the Buyer and Seller regarding the quality or condition of the Items will thereafter be resolved through any Seller warranties, refunds, credits, mediation, or legal action.

The Seller that allows its Buyer time to pay is also called the AR "Originator," and the Buyer its "Account Debtor." The party that collects AR payments from the Buyer is called the "Servicer," a role the Seller normally performs, but which it may outsource to a third party. When a Seller grants its Buyer Credit Terms in the form of AR, it generally does not charge its Buyer any interest or fees, and either absorbs its funding costs as the price of doing business or passes them on to the Buyer by including them in its Item's price.

Seller AR Finance

Seller Creates AR by granting Buyer
30 days from delivery to pay for Items.

2

1 Seller delivers Items to Buyer.

SELLER

BUYER

3

Buyer pays for Items 30 days
after Item delivery.

Benefits to Seller Finance

- Buyer is granted time to pay for its Items, allowing it to use its available cash on hand to optimize its ongoing working capital.

- Seller gets paid on a schedule that meets its working capital needs (e.g., 30, 60, 90 days).

- Seller maintains or gains sales competitiveness by offering Credit Terms to existing or potential Buyers.

- Minimal documentation requirements for basic AR finance, requiring only a purchase order or sales agreement, and recording an open account AR on the Seller's books, invoicing the Buyer, and finally collecting and reconciling Buyer payments.

Seller's AR Financing Costs

- Credit Risk management costs, including costs to procure and analyze Buyer credit information, delinquent payment recovery costs, unrecovered losses, and the cost of any TCI, or other risk mitigation, procured for all or some of is AR.

- Seller's cost of capital for the duration of the Buyer's Credit Terms.

- Sellers may include AR financing costs in their prices to try to recoup those costs by passing them onto their Buyers.

Seller AR Financing Risks

- Losses caused by Buyer's nonpayment or protracted default due to Buyer's insolvency, financial distress, Commercial Risks, Economic Risks, or Political Risks.

- Seller maintaining an ineffective Buyer Credit Risk management process that results in losses due to it providing Credit Terms to uncreditworthy Buyers.

- Seller maintaining an overly restrictive Buyer Credit Risk management process that results in limiting its competitiveness and losing sales due to it restricting sales to only the most creditworthy Buyers.

- Fraud by selling to a Buyer that has no intention of paying the AR.

- Compliance Risks, violating laws or regulations (e.g., anti-money laundering, contraband goods, selling to a sanctioned Buyer) resulting in fines or unenforceable Trade Debt.

- Currency fluctuation risks when Sellers agree to extend Credit Terms in foreign currencies.

SELLER AR RISK MITIGATION STRATEGIES

Self-Insurance

Most Sellers self-insure against their AR financing risks, using their own in-house Credit Risk management process to assess their Buyers' creditworthiness. A Seller's Credit Risk management process typically includes relying on its own assessment of Buyer payment histories, reviewing credit references from other Sellers, researching and reviewing Buyer financial statements, or reviewing credit reports from credit reporting agencies or TC Insurers. When Buyer credit reports, financial statements, or credit references are not available, a Seller will either demand cash at delivery, decline the Trade, or accept the Credit and other risks.

TCI or PRI

Sellers can purchase TCI or PRI to cover 80% to 95% of the value of their AR losses resulting from Buyer nonpayment due to insolvency, protracted default, or Political Risks. TCI and PRI Costs, including flat fees and annual premium rates are generally based on the TCI or PRI Insurer's Credit Risk assessment of the covered Buyers, and the total dollar amount of coverage. When covering all or most of a Seller's portfolio of Buyers, annual premiums and fees are typically calculated based on the Seller's projected gross annual sales revenues from the covered Buyers. Alternatively, premiums may be calculated based on a fixed Credit Limit assigned to each covered Buyer.

TCI Contract Between Insurer and Seller Covering Buyer's AR Payment Risk

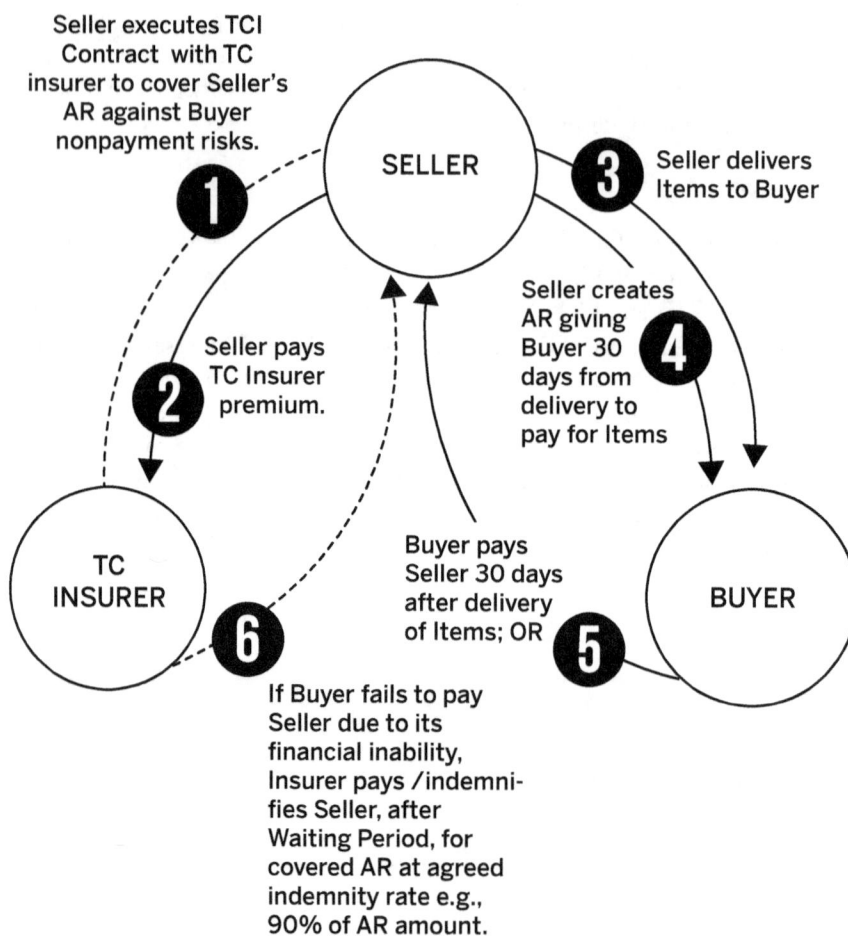

Seller executes TCI Contract with TC insurer to cover Seller's AR against Buyer nonpayment risks.

1

SELLER

3 Seller delivers Items to Buyer

Seller pays TC Insurer premium.

2

Seller creates AR giving Buyer 30 days from delivery to pay for Items

4

TC INSURER

6

Buyer pays Seller 30 days after delivery of Items; OR

5

BUYER

If Buyer fails to pay Seller due to its financial inability, Insurer pays /indemnifies Seller, after Waiting Period, for covered AR at agreed indemnity rate e.g., 90% of AR amount.

Selling AR

Sellers may mitigate their AR financing risks by selling all or part of their AR, or any other form of their Buyer's Trade Debt, to other Financiers, typically in exchange for immediate cash less a discount for the Financier's interest charges.

Third-Party Payment Guarantees and Standby Letters of Credit

A Seller may mitigate its AR financing risks by requiring its Buyer to provide a creditworthy third-party (e.g., bank, Buyer's parent or affiliate, or government) unconditional payment Guarantee or a Standby LC issued by a bank. Sellers may resort to third-party guarantees in cases where the Buyer is unknown to it or whose Credit Risk is deemed too high for the Seller to accept, or where TCI or PRI is not available, too costly, or comes with too many conditions or exclusions. The Buyer will pay the Standby LC Issuing Bank fees based on the Buyer's creditworthiness. The fees will typically be calculated as a per quarter or per annum rate, based on the average daily amount available to be drawn under the LC, for each day during the LC Validity Period, plus possible LC drawing or other fees.

Foreign Currency Valuation Protection

Most cross-border Trade is denominated using US Dollars, with Euros being the second most used currency. For some Buyers in some countries, there are tax and other advantages to doing cross-border TF business in their local currencies. For example, Buyers may be prohibited from taking on debt in foreign currencies or may be subject to local withholding taxes or other charges on foreign currency debt payments. Their foreign Sellers may be willing to accept AR payments in the Buyer's local currency if there is a foreign exchange market that allows the Seller to purchase from a Financier a "foreign exchange forward" that enables it to lock in an acceptable local currency exchange rate that will take effect when the Buyer makes its local currency payment, thus ensuring it can exchange its local currency into sufficient US Dollars or Euros to cover the required AR payment amount. For example, on the day the Seller delivers to its Buyer in Turkey Items for $1 mm (USD), it creates an AR on its books for $1 mm (USD) payable in 30 days, and invoices the Buyer for 6,000,000 Turkish Lira (TRY).[15] On that same day, the Seller buys from a Financier a TRY/USD forward contract in which the Seller promises to deliver the Financier TRY 6,000,000 in 30 days in exchange for the Financier agreeing to deliver the Seller $1 mm (USD) on that day. The Seller will pass the cost of the foreign exchange forward to the Buyer, usually in the Items' price. This use of foreign exchange forwards for short-term AR allows the Seller to win and keep new business by offering local currency invoicing to Buyers and allows its Buyers to reap whatever local currency financing benefits they may. Moreover, this solution also enables Financiers to purchase foreign currency AR from these Sellers without the foreign currency risk.

---

15   Turkish Lira to US Dollar exchange rates used in the example are purely for illustration purposes and do not reflect actual exchange rates.

RECEIVABLE - AR PURCHASE FINANCE

AR Purchase Finance (aka "Open Account Finance," "Factoring," or "Invoice Discounting") is one of the leading types of both domestic and international Financier-provided TF used throughout the world. It involves a Financier, usually a bank or other specialist finance company, purchasing a Seller's AR with the rights to its Buyers' payments, and the Financier having little or no recourse to the Seller for losses, except those due to Trade Disputes, Dilution, or fraud by a party to the transaction. There is no difference between "factoring," "invoice discounting," or other forms of AR Purchase Finance. The term "factoring" is often used in Europe and some other countries and has typically been associated with financing done for specific industries (e.g., the garment industry in the USA).

Financiers are generally in the business of purchasing only diverse portfolios of AR that are payable by different Buyers so they can diversify their Credit and other risks. Exceptionally, Financiers may agree to purchase one or more AR that are payable by a single or small group of Buyers (5 or under), despite the concentration of risk, especially if the AR are insured by TCI or are payable by highly creditworthy Buyers.

The price the Financier will pay the Seller for each AR will be equal to its percentage share (e.g., 90% or 100%) of the total amount (e.g., Invoice Amount) due from the Buyer, less the Financier's financing costs (interest and any fees). For example, if the Seller is owed $100 from its Buyer and the Financier buys 100% of that AR, it will pay the Seller a price of $100, minus its interest and fees.

Seller Benefits

- Mitigates all or part of its Buyer payment risks.

- Improves working capital and cash flow management by accelerating sales recognition, reducing the number of days sales are outstanding (DSO), by turning AR more quickly into cash to be used to fund its operations and reduce the need for external borrowing.

- Reduces working capital costs when the Financier charges the Seller less in interest and fees than the Seller's borrowing costs.

- Potential to increase sales to new and existing Buyers by offering Credit Terms without accompanying payment risks.

Financier Benefits

- AR Buyer payment risk mitigation is widely available. Financiers can purchase TCI or PRI to cover 80% to 100% of the value of its purchased AR against the risks of Buyer nonpayment. The TCI market has historically had ample capacity to insure AR debt, and using TCI enables Financiers to arrange significantly greater volumes of TF relative to their Credit Risk capacity.

- Involves taking preferred short-term risks. AR Purchase Finance requires taking only short-term risks, rather than medium- or long-term ones, which are generally considered to be riskier because Credit and other risks tend to increase over time. TF Financiers typically prefer short-term Credit Periods, which allow them to redeploy their capital depending on current market conditions.

- Uncommitted facilities available. It is very common for a Financier's AR Purchase agreements to be *uncommitted*, or subject to numerous conditions (e.g., availability of TCI, etc.), which effectively gives a Financier wide discretion whether to make any AR Purchases or to modify AR Purchase conditions based on changing market conditions.

- Does not interfere with the Seller's Asset-Based Loans. Financiers can purchase AR that the Seller has already pledged as collateral to secure loans from asset-based Financiers. Doing so may require the Seller to obtain an agreement from its asset-based Financiers in exchange for the Seller promising to apply its AR sales proceeds first towards repaying any outstanding or past due Asset-Based Loan balances. It should be in the interests of an asset-based Financier to agree to this arrangement, since it will result in turning its AR collateral into cash without the AR nonpayment risks.

- Stable source of financing. AR Purchase Finance is a relatively stable source of short-term credit that Financiers have been able to provide when traditional credit markets deteriorate or become scarce or too expensive. For example, during the 2008 financial crisis, medium- and long-term credit for all but the most creditworthy Obligors became scarce and expensive. AR Purchase Finance, however, was still widely available by the Financiers who were already in the business of providing it.

- Has broad application for both domestic or cross-border Trade, for businesses of any size, and can be administered as a low- or high-tech solution, depending on transaction sizes.

Potential Disadvantages of AR Purchase Finance

- **Costs:** A Seller's cost of selling its AR may become uneconomical after taking into consideration the Financier's interest charges and fees, and the cost of any TCI or other risk mitigation.

- **Possible TCI or PRI Cancellation:** Transactions that are subject to the purchased AR being TCI or PRI insured can be cancelled quickly if TC Insurers decide to cancel or modify coverage. Even transactions for which "non-cancellable" insurance is procured come with numerous conditions that can effectively prevent AR from being covered (e.g., requiring the Seller to cease shipments to past due Buyers, imposing material adverse information reporting requirements, etc.)

- **Extra Work and Expense:** Selling AR requires extra work by the Seller in the form of procuring and negotiating an economical transaction with a Financier and then administering it as well as organizing and transmitting its AR to the

Financier for each sale on a daily, weekly, or monthly schedule. There are, however, numerous technologies that can help automate much of this work, which are described in more detail in Chapter 7.

- **Uncommitted Facilities:** Sellers may be denied AR sales if market or Buyer conditions change. Financiers could also end up wasting time and money establishing AR Purchase programs that go unused by the Seller, which is why Financiers may decide to charge a Seller some minimum program setup fee.

- **Possibly Disrupting Seller-Buyer Relationships:** Financiers may require the Seller to notify their Buyers about their sale of AR to ensure that Buyer payments are sent to the agreed collections account in order to avoid mistaken or deliberate misdirection of AR payments. Sellers, however, may not want to notify their Buyers of the AR sales, as it may be interpreted by their Buyers as a lack of trust in their creditworthiness, or a Buyer may simply not want a new third-party Financier involved in its commercial relationship with its Seller.

AR Purchase Finance Structure

AR Origination

A Seller delivers Items to one or more Buyers, creating AR by giving each Buyer 30 or more days after delivery to pay and recording each AR as an open account on its accounting books and records, thereby creating a portfolio of AR potentially eligible for sale to a Financier.

Selecting a Financier to Purchase AR

The Seller will seek, from one or more Financiers, the most favorable terms and conditions for selling its AR. Sellers will generally have a portfolio of AR to sell, payable by a diverse group of Buyers, that will likely be diversified in terms of Credit Risks, amounts, and domestic vs. foreign. Some Financiers have greater Credit Risk capacity than others for certain types of Buyers, industries, geographies, transaction sizes, or other criteria. A Seller will, therefore, try to select a Financier that has the Credit Risk appetite to purchase as much of its AR as possible so that it can avoid having to retain, and not sell, a large portion of its AR, and avoid having to sell its AR to multiple Financiers. Its selection of a Financier will depend on:

a) the number of AR the Financier is willing to purchase based on its risk and balance sheet capacity.

b) its interest charges and fees.

c) frequency of permitted AR sales (daily, weekly, monthly).

d) whether the Financier provides a technology platform that makes AR sales efficient, simple, and cost-effective for the Seller.

e) The Financier's expertise and customer service standards.

Financier's AR Review

A prospective Financier will review the Seller's AR portfolio and its Buyers' credit-worthiness to determine which AR it is willing to purchase and its pricing and other terms. Depending on the number of Buyers in the portfolio, a Financier may review each Buyer's creditworthiness or, to save time when reviewing large portfolios (e.g., 30 or more Buyers), review only those Buyers that account for the majority of the Seller's AR amounts (e.g., 70% to 80%). Financiers may also supplement their review data by obtaining TCI quotes for all or some of the AR from TC Insurers that typically have better Credit and other data for analyzing and pricing AR portfolios quickly. AR payable by Buyers that may be deemed creditworthy by the Financier but which reside, or do a substantial amount of business, in countries that involve excessive Political, Legal, Compliance, or other Risks, will likely be deemed ineligible and excluded from purchase.

AR Purchase Agreement Negotiation

The Financier and Seller will typically negotiate and agree to the key terms of their proposed AR Purchase transaction in the form of an "indicative," nonbinding Term Sheet, after which they will enter into a formal, legally binding, written Receivables Purchase Agreement (RPA). The RPA will be structured to include the various terms and conditions to satisfy each party's needs and objectives, and Buyers are not normally a party to RPAs and might never become aware that their Seller is selling AR unless the RPA requires that they be notified.

Standard RPA Terms:

- The Validity Period is the time period within which the Financier is willing to purchase AR and is typically one year, or less in cases of one-off AR Purchases.

- List of Buyers eligible for purchase, and their respective Buyer Credit Limits, stating the maximum amount of each Buyer's AR payment risk to which the Financier is willing to be exposed at any time during the Validity Period (e.g., Buyer X's Credit Limit = $3 mm, Buyer Y's Credit Limit = $1 mm).

- The Facility Amount is the maximum, aggregate, Dollar amount of all AR payment risk to which the Financier is willing to be exposed at any one time (e.g., $100 mm maximum).

- Percentage of each AR the Financier agrees to purchase (e.g., 100%, 95%, 90%) and the unpurchased percentage to be retained by the Seller.

- Application of AR Payments: AR payments may be applied first to the Financier or pro rata according to their ownership share in each AR. Pro rata application of payments will provide stronger support for the Financier's position, if challenged in a court of law, that its purchase of AR in which the Seller retains a minority interest nevertheless meets the standard of a legal true sale (as described further below). Otherwise, depending on applicable laws, the legal true sale requirements may not be met if the Financier has full recourse to the Seller for its retained share of the AR.

- Maximum AR payment periods (e.g., 30, 60, 90 days).
- Required TCI coverage, if any, or other form of risk mitigation that must be in place as a condition of each AR Purchase, and the party that is responsible for procuring and administering it.
- Permitted frequency of each AR Purchase (e.g., daily, weekly, monthly, or quarterly).
- Financier's interest or discount rate, and any fees it may charge.
- Designation of the Servicer (e.g., Seller, Financier, or third party) and its responsibilities, and the ownership and location of the AR collections account.
- The RPA will state that the Seller is required to repurchase any AR that goes unpaid and is deemed ineligible for purchase under the terms of the RPA, including Trade Disputes, Dilution, or Seller's or Buyer's fraud.
- Seller's representations and warranties that the AR being sold will meet the conditions of the parties' RPA and its other obligations under the RPA.

Servicing

The RPA should state whether the Seller, Financier, or some other third party will Service the AR. The Servicer will have access to and administer a separate AR payment collections account into which the Buyers' payments will be made. The Servicer will apply AR payments to first cover any Servicing Fees that are due, then the Financier's interest and principal amounts due as well as any amounts owing to the Seller if it retained any ownership percentage the AR. The collection account will be opened and owned by either the Seller or the Financier, or by one of their affiliated businesses. It is common for the collections account to be a single purpose account in which the Seller's or Financier's other funds are not at risk of being commingled with the Financier's AR payments. Using a separate collections account can also be important in case the Financier has to prove to a bankruptcy court or some other party that it, rather than the Seller, owns the AR payments in that account. However, in some cases that involve large, very creditworthy Sellers, the Financier may allow the Seller to be the Servicer without the need to establish a separate collections account.

Legal True Sale

An essential element to an AR Purchase transaction is that the Financier takes legally recognized ownership to the portion of each AR it is purchasing, rather than simply taking a security interest in the AR as loan collateral. This is a critical distinction for protecting a Financier against a Seller's bankruptcy risk and for purposes of enforcing any TCI covering purchased AR. If a Financier's AR Purchase transaction becomes recharacterized by a bankruptcy or other legal authority as a secured loan, the purchased AR becomes subject to any superior claims made by the Seller's other creditors (e.g., a Seller's asset-based Lender). A Seller's asset-based Lender will typically record its security interests in its loan collateral in public records in a legally recognized manner, such as the Uniform Commercial

Code (UCC) used throughout the United States. Financiers that purchase AR in the United States will typically also record their security interests in their purchased AR as an added safety measure in case their AR Purchase transaction is recharacterized as a secured loan by a bankruptcy court or other legal authority. Additionally, for purposes of making valid claims for TCI coverage on the AR, the insured party must own the covered AR. This means the Financier that purchased the AR must be the legal owner of it to be able to make a claim under its TCI Contract. Any TCI the Seller may have covering its AR is terminated once it sells that AR to a Financier. In other words, the TCI does not attach and follow the AR to its new owners. This often overlooked requirement for the insured to have an insurable ownership interest in a TCI-covered AR.

To achieve a degree of certainty on whether the Financier takes legal ownership to its purchased AR, a Financier may obtain a "true sale" legal opinion from its attorneys confirming that its AR Purchase meets the true sale legal requirements under applicable laws. Under most State laws in the United States, legal true sale requirements are satisfied when the Financier has no, very limited, or permissible recourse against the Seller for AR nonpayments. A limited or permissible level of recourse generally allows for the Financier to require the Seller to repurchase AR or the portion of it which is not legally enforceable due to a Trade Dispute, Dilution or fraud. Some jurisdictions in the United States and other countries may deem it a true legal sale when the Financier maintains some relatively small level of permissible pro rata risk sharing or recourse against the Seller for a Buyer's failure to pay due to its financial inability to pay. It is also important to know that under the laws of virtually every State in the United States, AR Purchases in which the Financier has *full recourse* against the Seller for AR nonpayment due a Buyer's financial inability to pay are considered loans and not legal true sales of AR, irrespective of what the parties may intend or state to the contrary in their RPA. It should also be noted that an attorney's true sale legal opinion is often highly qualified by the attorney providing it, and in no way constitutes a Guarantee that the AR sale will not be successfully challenged in a bankruptcy or other court. It is also not uncommon for Financiers to structure and execute their AR Purchase transactions based on their custom, practice, and confidence in their own expertise, without obtaining true sale legal opinions.

Accounting True Sale

A Seller that wants to ensure that it achieves all of its anticipated off-balance sheet accounting benefits for selling its AR, such as early sales recognition and reduced DSO, may have its accountants provide an "accounting true sale" opinion confirming that its AR sales will be recognized as such in its accounting books and records. The Seller's applicable accounting standards will be used in making this determination. In the US, at the time of this writing, the accounting analysis would rely on the Financial Accounting Standards Board's (FASB) and the US. Generally Accepted Accounting Principles (GAAP). For Sellers in Europe, at the time of this writing, the accounting analysis may apply the International Accounting Standards Board's (IASB) or the Financial Reporting Standards (IFRS) practices.

A similar level of analysis used for determining a legal true sale concerning the amount of any recourse the Financier retains against the Seller for unpaid AR is performed to confirm an accounting true sale, but with more emphasis on applicable accounting practices and rules. The Seller's accountants may consider any legal true sale opinions issued by the Seller's or other attorneys, but an accounting true sale opinion is not the same as a legal true sale opinion. A Financier, for example, may rely on its attorney's legal true sale opinion to find comfort that its AR Purchases would likely survive legal challenges, while the Seller's accountants may determine that the transaction, nevertheless, fails to satisfy its accounting true sale requirements. This possible divergence in accounting and legal true sale opinions does not necessarily nullify or undermine either opinion's usefulness or either party's willingness to execute the transaction. The Seller's accountants may simply be acting cautiously in general, or the transaction structure may be too complex or untested to provide the necessary level of accounting certainty.

Notifying Buyers of AR Sales

In some cases, a Financier may require the Seller to notify its Buyers that it is selling its AR to a Financier. This notification may be used to mitigate the risk of the Seller directing its Buyers to make payments to an account other than the agreed collections account. According to laws in certain countries, notified Buyers become legally required to submit their payments to the designated Financier as a condition to discharging their debt.

Committed vs. Uncommitted RPA

A Seller will generally prefer to have the Financier unconditionally commit in the RPA that it will purchase AR that meet the parties' agreed criteria, whether or not the Financier wishes to change its mind during the RPA's Validity Period. Without such a committed RPA, the Financier would have total discretion whether to purchase AR or to change the terms, which it would likely do in case the AR nonpayment or other risks increase. For committed RPAs, Financiers will typically charge the Seller a commitment fee and impose some conditions, such as a requirement that during any RPA Validity Period—in the opinion of the Financier—no material adverse changes occur to a Buyer's creditworthiness; the Seller's bankruptcy risk; market, political, compliance, or regulatory risks; or other circumstances that may result in losses or harm to the Financier. Except in times of severe market changes or a financial crisis, most Financiers would not be expected to exercise their "material adverse change" capriciously or irrationally to suspend all AR Purchases after having spent the effort and resources to arrange, document, and execute the transaction. It would, however, likely suspend purchasing specific AR for which the Buyer's payment risk has materially changed.

Financier's Interest Rate

The Financier will charge the Seller an interest rate based on the formula agreed to in their RPA. It will comprise the Financier's cost of funds plus its "Margin," which should be commensurate with the Credit and other risks it is taking. A Financier's cost of funds comprises its cost of acquiring capital, any regulatory capital costs imposed on the amounts it puts at risk in a transaction, and its business overhead costs. Chapter 5 provides a more detailed explanation of how TF in general is funded. The Financier's cost of funds will be determined on, or in some cases two days prior to, the date of each AR Purchase and will fluctuate based on movements in the interest rate market. The Financier's Margin, however, should remain fixed, unless the parties renegotiate it due to changes in the AR payment or other risks. If the Financier is to purchase a portfolio of AR in which some Buyer' risks vary widely, it may agree to charge the Seller a range of different interest rates according to each AR's risks.

Interest will be charged on the amount of the Financier's funds at risk for the number of days the AR go unpaid. If the Financier's interest is to be paid at the time of each AR Purchase, it is called a "discount rate," and will be deducted from the Financier's purchase price paid to the Seller. Alternatively, a Financier could agree to charge the Seller interest in "arrears," after the Buyer makes its payment. Interest paid in arrears, however, may make the AR Purchase appear more like a secured loan in which interest is always paid in arrears, rather than a legal true sale of AR, and thus many Financiers will prefer to use the discount method of collecting interest.

Example:
To purchase an AR that is payable in 30 days, the Financier may charge the Seller an interest rate equal to its cost of funds using the one-month London Interbank Bank Rate (LIBOR) or SOFR, published one or two days prior to the AR Purchase (e.g., 2% p.a.) plus the Financier's Margin (e.g., 4% p.a.), resulting in a total interest rate of 6% per annum. If the Financier purchases 100% of a $1000 Receivable due in 30 days, the Financier would pay the Seller $970. That is the $1000 Receivable value, minus the Financier's discount rate of $5, based on an interest rate of 6% per annum ($60 for one full year divided by 12 months = $5 per month of interest).

Charging Interest for Late Buyer AR Payments
Sometimes Buyers pay late, which creates interest payment shortfalls for Financiers that collect their interest using the discount method. Therefore, the parties need to agree in the RPA how to collect interest for late Buyer payments. A common way to collect late interest is to have the Financier add a pre-agreed fixed number of extra "grace days" to each AR's due dates when it calculates and collects each discount rate. For example, if a Buyer's payments are due in 30 days, but historically it pays on average 5 days late, the Financier would add 5 "grace days" to each discount interest rate calculation. Another alternative is for the Financier to collect late interest from the Seller or the Buyers in arrears after the exact late payment interest charges are known.

Financier Fees
The Financier may also charge Sellers up-front or recurring periodic fees to cover its cost of establishing or administering the transaction, or to cover its opportunity

AR Purchase Finance – Financier Purchasing AR From Seller

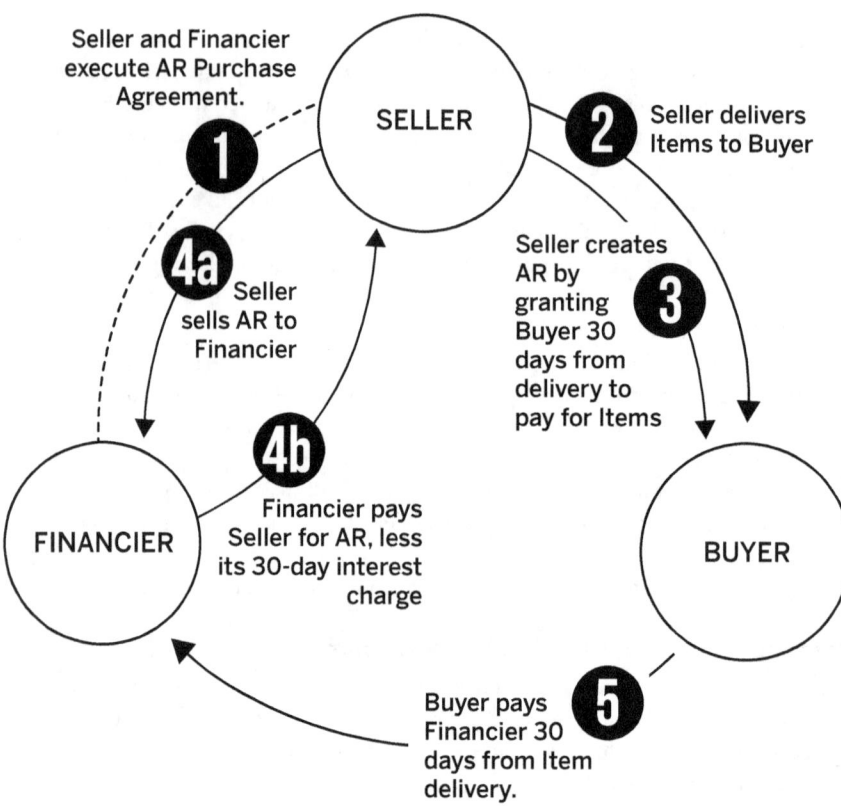

Seller and Financier execute AR Purchase Agreement.

1

2 Seller delivers Items to Buyer

SELLER

Seller creates AR by granting Buyer 30 days from delivery to pay for Items

3

4a Seller sells AR to Financier

4b Financier pays Seller for AR, less its 30-day interest charge

FINANCIER

BUYER

Buyer pays Financier 30 days from Item delivery.

5

costs associated with reserving its credit and risk capacity during the RPA Validity Period, or simply as a source of additional transaction revenue with no relation to its fixed or other costs. For example, the Financier may charge an up-front RPA setup fee (e.g., a Facility fee) equal to 1% of the RPA Facility Amount. It may also charge a commitment fee equal to some percentage (e.g., 1%) of the unused Facility Amount, calculated and payable monthly in advance or arrears.

The Servicer will charge Servicing Fees to either the Financier or Seller for its work administering, collecting, and reconciling AR payments. This fee will be based on the anticipated or actual amount of Servicing work done during the billing period and is typically calculated and billed monthly or quarterly.

Funding AR Purchase Transactions

To fund its AR Purchases, a Financier will use either its own capital, funds borrowed from lenders, or funds raised from debt obligations it may issue, such as bonds or commercial paper. The interest or discount rate the Financier charges a Seller will comprise its cost of funds plus its risk Margin.

In an RPA, the Financier's cost of funds used in its interest or discount rate formula, to which it will add its Margin, will normally be a published, *variable,* Interest Reference Rate rather than a rate formula the Financier determines at its sole discretion. If the cost of funds used in the RPA is lower than the Financier's actual cost of funds, it can try to make up the difference by increasing its Margin accordingly. Fixed interest rates are not normally used in RPAs, because establishing one typically requires using interest rate derivatives, swaps, and options that add unnecessary complexity and costs due to the unpredictable timing and fluctuating funding amounts needed for each AR Purchase. The most common published variable US Dollar Interest Reference Rates used in AR Purchase transactions have been the London Interbank Offered Rate (LIBOR), the US Prime Rate, and the Fed Funds Rate (the target interest rate set by the Federal Open Market Committee (FOMC) at which commercial banks borrow and lend their excess reserves to each other overnight). For example, if the one-month LIBOR or SOFR is selected as the Interest Reference Rate, then on the day of each AR Purchase, the one-month LIBOR or SOFR in effect on that date plus the Financier's Margin is used to calculate the Seller's total interest or discount rate. AR Purchases funded in other currencies will use Interest Reference Rates published for those currencies, for example, the one-month Euribor.

AR Purchase Finance Risks

Buyer Payment Default

Payment default arises from a Buyer's nonpayment, late payment, or protracted default due to a Buyer's inability to pay. Protracted default means a Buyer is making partial or no payments over a protracted period of time (e.g., more than. 60 days) without formally declaring bankruptcy or filing for bankruptcy protection. In these cases, the Buyer may be selectively paying certain Sellers, employees, or other debts and is either waiting for its cash flow to improve in order to pay its debts, or it is simply winding down its business. AR nonpayment risks are borne by the Financier according to its share of each purchased AR.

Trade Disputes

A Trade Dispute occurs when a Buyer refuses to pay for all or part of the Items that it claims do not conform to its Trade agreement and the Seller *disagrees* and believes the Items do conform. This risk is borne by the Seller because Trade Disputes nullify the Seller's legal claim for payment against the Buyer, and the AR must be repurchased from the Financier because it is not legally enforceable.

Dilution

Dilution occurs when Buyer refuses to pay for all or part of the Items that it claims do not conform to the parties' Trade agreement and the Seller *agrees*. This risk is borne by the Seller, since it lessens the value of its legal claim for payment against the Buyer. Dilution arises in the normal course of business and is not necessarily a sign that things have gone seriously wrong. Dilution is typically handled by the Seller either reimbursing the Financier for the diluted AR amount or the Buyer agreeing to pay the full AR amount, including the diluted portion, on the condition that the Seller provides the Buyer a credit equal to the diluted amount, applicable to the Buyer's next purchase, which may be documented as a "credit memo."

Seller or Buyer Fraud

Fraud occurs when either the Seller or Buyer, or both in concert, defraud the Financier by having it purchase AR for which there is either no actual Buyer or no actual Trade, or where the Buyer takes delivery of Items with no intention of paying for them. This risk is borne by the Financier, unless it can enforce its rights and successfully recover its losses from the Seller or Buyer.

Breach of RPA

An RPA breach occurs when one party fails to honor any of its contractual obligations in the RPA, resulting in losses or harm to another party. This can occur when market changes make the RPA unprofitable or impossible to honor. For example, a Seller that is under financial stress may decide to breach the RPA by directing its Buyers to pay the Seller directly rather than paying the collections account, or if the Seller is also the Servicer, by applying collected funds to pay its employees or critical vendors in order to survive. Financiers may breach their RPA obligations by failing to purchase AR it was legally committed to purchase in order to avoid purchasing AR that it determines has become too risky.

Legal True Sale Reclassification Risks

Whenever a Financier purchases less than 100% of an AR, or retains some form of recourse against the Seller, it risks not satisfying legal true sale requirements and thus exposes itself to the Seller's bankruptcy risk and the risk of any TCI coverage being voided. To avoid this risk, the Financier and its attorneys may structure the RPA and any residual Seller recourse in a manner consistent with legal true sale laws in effect in the legal jurisdiction governing the transaction. Successful legal true sale structures involving Seller risk sharing or recourse evolve and change over time and may be different depending on applicable laws.

Seller True Sale Accounting Risks

A Seller's accountants may deem its sale of AR as a secured loan, rather than an accounting true sale, thus depriving the Seller of any accounting benefits such as reducing its days sales are outstanding (DSO), early sales recognition, or Buyer payment risk transfer.

Compliance and Legal Risks

When the Trade underlying an AR is illegal or not in compliance with applicable laws or regulations (e.g., anti-money laundering, contraband goods, sanctioned parties), the parties to the RPA may be prohibited by law from enforcing their transaction or the AR against the Buyer, or the parties may be exposed to fines or penalties from government authorities. For example, if a Financier purchases an AR for which the Buyer or one its owners or investors is on a government-issued sanctions list, the Financier could be legally exposed and subject to fines for implementing that AR Purchase or for collecting any Buyer payments. The affected AR would also become ineligible for TCI coverage and could prevent the payment of any claims.

Financier Funding Risks

A Financier's funding costs could rise over time, due to economic changes or a deterioration of its creditworthiness, to a point that makes its transactions unaffordable for one or both of the parties. For example, if the Financier is downgraded and can no longer fund itself at or near its agreed Interest Reference Rate (e.g., LIBOR or SOFR), it will have to either negotiate an increased interest rate with its Sellers or cancel its transactions. This problem occurred for many banks during the 2008/2009 financial crisis, when many of them lost the ability to fund at or near LIBOR in the short or long term. To help address these risks, RPAs can be structured to leave the parties some flexibility to modify their funding costs and agree to alternative funding formulas, or at least limit the funding cost increases that can be passed on to a Seller.

Mitigating AR Purchase Finance Risks

Many, if not most, of the TF risks outlined earlier in this material can be mitigated with risk mitigation tools or through structuring the transaction to share or reallocate those risks to third parties that are in the business of taking them. Below are the most used and effective forms of AR Purchase Finance risk mitigation.

Trade Credit Insurance

Sellers or Financiers can purchase TCI to cover up to 100% of the value of their AR payments against the risk of Buyer nonpayment due to its insolvency or protracted default. There is ample capacity in the TCI market, making it the most reliable, stable, and cost-effective risk mitigation tool for AR Purchase Finance. RPAs that require purchased AR be covered by TCI are very common among Financiers for the following reasons:

- TCI substantially reduces the Financier's risk of Buyer nonpayment by substituting it with a TC Insurer's, most of which are rated A or above, which is higher than most Buyers' ratings.

- TCI saves the Financier substantial time and costs that it would otherwise have to spend assessing the creditworthiness of each Buyer, about which it may possess very little or no financial information.

Managing a TCI Contract in coordination with an RPA can be complicated and requires a fair degree of expertise and attention. Accordingly, unless the Seller's AR are already TC Insured, most Financiers will want to purchase their own TCI Contract to maintain close control over its operation. If, however, the Seller's AR are already TC Insured, or the Seller insists on being an insured party, the only way for the Financier's purchased AR to be insured is to have the TCI Contract name the Financier as the insured or co-insured, or by having the policy state that the Seller's insurable interest in the AR is transferrable to other parties, including the Financier, upon sale of its insured AR. A TCI insured must maintain ownership of the Trade Debt insured under its Contract, which in legal terms is called its "insurable interest." If the insured sells the insured Trade Debt, it will no longer be insured. Merely having the Financier named in the Seller's TCI Contract as a "loss payee" is not sufficient because, according to most TCI Contracts, once an insured AR is sold, it is no longer insured because only the original insured or co-insured party, not subsequent AR purchasers, can have a covered "insurable interest" in its AR. This important fact is not always understood or known by AR Financiers but is a critical issue that should be addressed by the Financier directly with the TC Insurer (not just the Broker) to ensure that the proposed TCI will in fact cover the AR as expected.

Matching AR Purchase Transaction with TCI Contract

Financiers using TCI must read and understand their TCI Contract details to be certain that its coverage matches exactly the nonpayment or other risks it intends to be covered in its transaction. A properly worded TCI Contract issued for an AR Purchase transaction will state clearly that it covers only losses resulting from nonpayment of a Seller's legally enforceable AR, so long as the Contract's other conditions are also satisfied. Unless stated otherwise, TCI Contracts will not cover other "trade related" losses. For example, a Financier's losses arising from a Seller failing to honor its RPA obligations, representations, or warranties will not be covered.

TCI Contract Between Insurer and Financier Purchasing AR From Seller Covering Buyer AR Nonpayment Risks

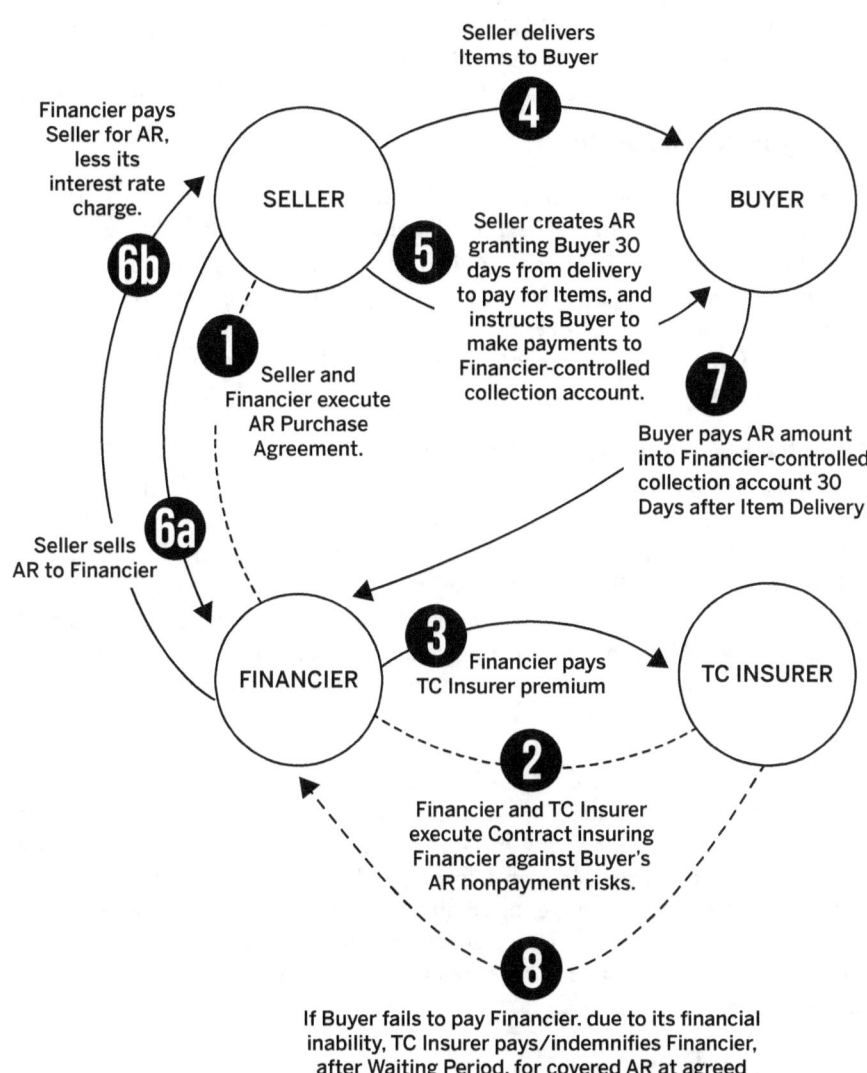

Seller delivers Items to Buyer

4

SELLER

BUYER

Financier pays Seller for AR, less its interest rate charge.

6b

Seller creates AR granting Buyer 30 days from delivery to pay for Items, and instructs Buyer to make payments to Financier-controlled collection account.

5

1

Seller and Financier execute AR Purchase Agreement.

7

Buyer pays AR amount into Financier-controlled collection account 30 Days after Item Delivery

Seller sells AR to Financier

6a

FINANCIER

3

Financier pays TC Insurer premium

TC INSURER

2

Financier and TC Insurer execute Contract insuring Financier against Buyer's AR nonpayment risks.

8

If Buyer fails to pay Financier. due to its financial inability, TC Insurer pays/indemnifies Financier, after Waiting Period, for covered AR at agreed indemnity rate, e.g., 90% of AR amount

A common area for TCI coverage mismatch can occur when a Financier procures TCI to cover AR it purchases on a *full recourse* basis to the Seller. In a full recourse AR Purchase transaction, the Financier does not acquire ownership or legal title to the AR, nor the critical "insurable interest" in the AR, and therefore its TCI Contract will not cover losses due to nonpayment of the AR. To avoid this mismatch, the Financier needs to acknowledge to the Insurer that it is making a secured loan to the Seller, collateralized with the Seller's AR that it wants to have covered by TCI. In this case, the Insurer will either make the Financier and Seller co-insureds or make the Seller the sole insured with the Financier a loss payee with a power of attorney giving the Financier the right to file claims on the behalf of the Seller.

Trade Disputes and Dilution

Trade Dispute and Dilution risks may be mitigated by the Seller or a Financier requiring a Buyer to document its Trade Payable as a Negotiable Debt Instrument (e.g., Bill of Exchange) in which it waives any rights to claim Trade Disputes or Dilution as a reason for nonpayment. Most Buyers that have a choice of Sellers, however, are not likely to agree to such a requirement, unless they are receiving exceptional Credit Terms from the Seller or they are borrowing funds directly from a Financier that requires it.

Buyer Bankruptcy "Preference Payments"

In US bankruptcy cases, a Buyer's bankruptcy estate trustee has the power to require the return of certain Buyer payments made to its Sellers within 90 days prior to the Buyer's bankruptcy filing, if the payment was done in *preference* to that Seller over another similarly situated Seller. This preference payment risk exposes both the Seller and any Financier that purchases that Seller's AR to the risk of having to return AR payments. To mitigate this risk, the Seller or the Financier can purchase TCI that specifically covers bankruptcy preference payment risks.

Seller Insolvency

When a Seller of AR becomes insolvent or files for bankruptcy protection, the Financier that purchased its AR is at risk of (a) losing its ability to enforce against the Seller any representations or warranties, including any AR recourse obligations; and (b) having its ownership rights to its purchased AR and related payments challenged by the Seller's competing creditors that may argue the Financier did not acquire the AR by means of a legal true sale and that, therefore, the AR belongs in the Seller's bankruptcy estate to be shared among its creditors based the priority of their interests.

Legal Enforceability

There is a risk that purchased AR may not be legally enforceable against all or some of the Buyers according to the laws in the various legal jurisdictions in which the parties do business. This risk is rare in the course of normal domestic business and is more likely to occur with AR that are payable by foreign or publicly owned Buyers from countries with legal regimes that do not support AR Purchase Finance or that treat it differently than the Seller and Financier intended. This is also a critical issue to address for any TCI insured party, since AR that prove legally *unenforceable* are not covered under TCI Contracts. This legal enforceability risk can usually be addressed and mitigated by the concerned party, the Seller or Financier, receiving a legal opinion from an attorney confirming that the Buyers in question have the legal authority to contract as contemplated under relevant laws.

Fraud Risk

Fraud can occur in AR Purchase transactions in at least three ways. The most commons ways include when a Seller sells fictitious AR for which there is no Buyer; when a Seller instructs its Buyers to divert its payments to the Seller, instead of the Financier; and when the Seller or Buyer deceives the Financier as to the legality of its Trades and engages in illegal Trades (e.g., smuggling, selling to sanctioned parties, money laundering), which can result in the Financier being unable to collect AR payments or TCI claim payments.

To prevent these types of fraud, it is critical to engage in and maintain a robust KYC process that verifies the identity, location, and financial condition of each Buyer, and to not solely rely on the Seller's or a TC Insurer's due diligence. Additionally, Financiers can try to verify the authenticity of their AR with each Buyer by regularly or randomly asking each Buyer to confirm that the Seller's AR correspond to valid Trades. There are numerous AR management systems that automatically make these inquiries electronically on a periodic basis with real-time reporting. To prevent Sellers from instructing Buyers to divert their payments, Financiers may try requiring each Buyer to commit in writing that it will only take payment instructions from the Financier. Some Buyers, however, may not agree to make this commitment in writing since the Financier is not a party to its Trade with the Seller.

How Financiers May Achieve 100% TCI Coverage of Purchased AR

Most TC Insurers will require their insured party to share some level (e.g., 5% to 10%) of AR nonpayment risk to encourage the insured to stay engaged in its risk management. However, it is possible for a Financier to obtain 100% TCI coverage on its purchased AR by using one of the following structures:

1) The Financier may purchase only the insured portion (e.g., 95%) of each AR, leaving the risk of the uninsured portion (e.g., 5%) with the Seller. In this case, the Financier has to be careful to structure its AR Purchase in a way that meets legal true sale requirements, using a deferred purchase or other method, depending on the applicable true sale laws.

2) Alternatively, due to the highly competitive nature and evolution of the TCI market, some TC Insurers will provide Indemnity Rates as high as 100% for select transactions on the condition the Financier bears the risk of a first-loss Deductible at a rate that would be a fair substitute for the insured's normal share of retained risk (e.g., 5%). In such cases, if the TCI Contract imposes a first-loss Deductible of 5%, the Financier would

agree to purchase 100% of each AR from the Seller on the condition the Seller agrees to reimburse the Financier for any Deductible losses. The Seller's Deductible reimbursement obligation to the Financier may take the form of a payment Guarantee, Standby Letter of Credit, cash collateral held in a secure account, AR purchased on a deferred basis, or other means of security. Normally, TC Insurers will resist allowing an insured from recovering losses from other sources in addition to receiving the TCI claim payments. However, due to competition among TC Insurers, it has become a more common practice for TC Insurers to allow insureds to further cover their share of retained risk in this manner. Nevertheless, in all these cases, the TCI Contract should expressly state that the Financier is allowed to recover its losses from the Seller or other collateral without affecting the amount the Financier may collect under its TCI Contract.

3) The Financier can also mitigate its AR nonpayment risks through over-collateralization, pooling, or securitization by purchasing more AR than it actually funds, while deferring its payment to the Seller for those unfunded AR until after, and only if, the Buyer pays it for the AR it funded. For example, the Financier "buys" $12 mm of various AR, for which it pays the Seller only $8 mm, with a promise to pay the Seller the remaining $4 mm with any Buyer payments it receives over the $8 mm. Depending on applicable laws, however, this deferred payment structure may not produce a legal or accounting true sale because the Financier has full recourse to the Seller for a significant portion of the purchased AR ($4 mm). Nevertheless, it may be used effectively when either the applicable true sale laws support the structure or when neither party is concerned with having the transaction challenged by third parties.

A Financier may, however, achieve an accounting and legal true sale using *over-collateralization* to mitigate AR nonpayment risks by using a multistep *asset securitization* structure. There are numerous variations of AR asset securitization structures, all of which need to be carefully structured around different national or regional laws and financial accounting regulations. Nevertheless, the basic structure outlined below supports most AR asset securitization structures.

Step 1: A Seller sells its AR as a legal true sale, without recourse, to a special purpose, bankruptcy remote, legal entity (SPE). The SPE achieves bankruptcy remoteness by having its charter (a) restrict it from incurring any liabilities, thus removing the risk of and its ability to file for bankruptcy; and (b) requiring it to be maintained and operated as a separate business from any other company to which it may be affiliated, including the Seller, in order to prevent the SPE's assets from being consolidated with another company (e.g., the Seller's assets) in any bankruptcy proceeding. The SPE is often set up as a subsidiary of the Seller, and, to avoid its assets being consolidated with its parent, it must be established in a manner that satisfies specific accounting rules and tests, which are assessed and validated by specialized accountants. If the SPE's assets would be consolidated with the original Seller of AR, no legal or accounting true sale would be possible using this SPE structure.

Step 2: The SPE pays the Seller for its AR purchased in Step 1 with funds it either borrows from one or more Financiers or with funds it receives in exchange for selling its AR to one or more Financiers. TCI can be used to cover AR nonpayment risks for whichever party owns the insurable interest in the AR at the time of a claim, whether it is an SPE or a Financier that purchases the AR.

SUPPLY CHAIN FINANCE, (AKA CONFIRMED PAYABLES, REVERSE FACTORING, VENDOR FINANCE)

The term Supply Chain Finance, in its broadest sense, means any form of finance, TF or otherwise, that finances transactions among businesses involved in the production, sale, and delivery of Items along their respective supply chains. An Asset-Based Loan, for example, used by a Buyer to purchase raw materials is a form of non-TF Supply Chain Finance. However, in the TF industry, Supply Chain Finance (SCF) generally refers to a very specific type of TF structure in which a Buyer is granted extended payment terms (e.g., 30, 90, or 180 days) from its Sellers in exchange for the Buyer providing its Sellers the opportunity to sell their AR to the Buyer's Financier at an discount or interest rate based on the Buyer's creditworthiness. In an SCF structure, the Buyer agrees to "confirm" to the Financier that it will honor its payment obligations for each of its Trade Payables when they come due, excluding any that are diluted or disputed unless the Seller has granted the Buyer a credit for the diluted or disputed amount. This specific type of TF also goes by the names Confirmed Payables, Reverse Factoring, or Vendor Finance, depending on where the parties do business. It is referred to in this book simply as "SCF."

The Buyer's confirmation to the Financier—its confirmed Trade Payable—is intentionally stated as only a "confirmation" representing its intention to pay rather than a "promise" to pay. This is done to avoid creating a legal debt obligation for the Buyer to pay the Financier, which is necessary to avoid adversely affecting a Buyer's other creditor relationships, including any loan covenants or other debt agreements that restrict it from incurring additional debt. The Buyer's debt obligation to pay the Seller, however, remains unchanged and is represented by its Trade Payable and the Seller's corresponding AR.

SCF programs are generally arranged between a large, generally creditworthy Buyer, its Financier, and with as many Sellers the Buyer can convince to participate in its program. A Buyer with significant buying volumes can often leverage its market power to condition future purchases on a Seller's willingness to participate in the Buyer's SCF program. SCF programs can also be used to strengthen a Buyer's supply chain when its credit strength makes working capital more affordable for its Sellers that pay higher interest rates for their working capital than the interest rate charged by the Financier that buys its AR through the program.

SCF programs may be arranged to include any number of Sellers. Financiers managing SCF programs with large numbers of Sellers will typically use an in-house or third-party web-based technology platform to automate and administer their programs. Before purchasing any AR, the Financier must "on-board" each willing Seller as a participant in the SCF program. On-boarding a Seller involves the Financier conducting its KYC process, executing an RPA, and providing the Seller with instructions and transaction support for selling its AR.

The following is an example of how a basic SCF program works: (1) a Buyer and a Financier enter into an SCF agreement in which the Financier agrees to purchase AR from Sellers that are willing to grant the Buyer extended payment terms for which the Buyer has confirmed to the Financier its intention to pay; (2) the Buyer requests its Sellers to provide it with Credit Terms in which its AR is payable 90 days from delivery; (3) periodically (daily, weekly, etc.), the Buyer will transmit to the Financier a list of its confirmed Trade Payables (by Invoice or other format) that it intends pay on their respective due dates; (4) the Financier offers each on-boarded Seller the option of selling its AR to the Financier at an interest rate based on the Buyer's creditworthiness. Sellers have the option of selling their AR to the Financier or waiting to be paid directly by the Buyer on the 90-day due date; (5) the Financier collects purchased AR payments from the Buyer on their respective extended payment dates.

Supply Chain Finance, Confirmed Payables, Reverse Factoring

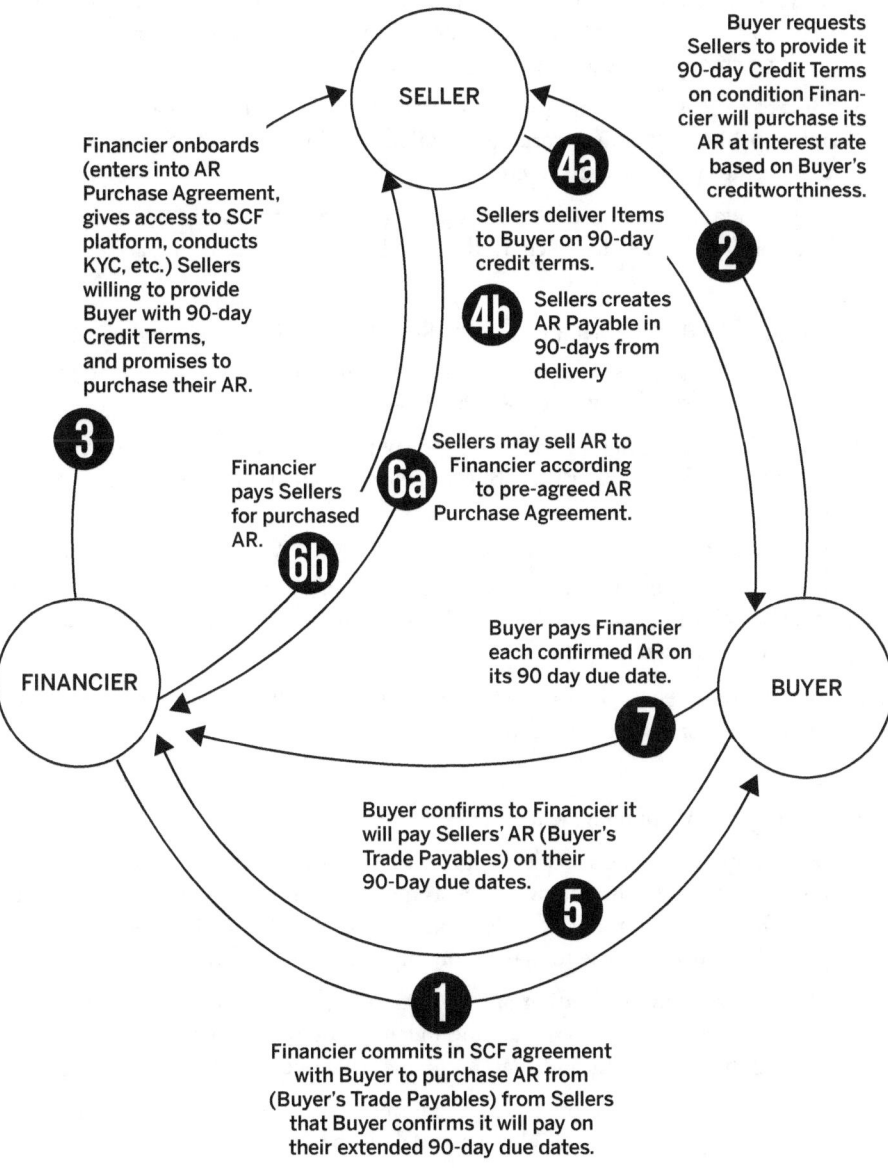

SELLER

Buyer requests Sellers to provide it 90-day Credit Terms on condition Financier will purchase its AR at interest rate based on Buyer's creditworthiness.

2

Financier onboards (enters into AR Purchase Agreement, gives access to SCF platform, conducts KYC, etc.) Sellers willing to provide Buyer with 90-day Credit Terms, and promises to purchase their AR.

3

4a Sellers deliver Items to Buyer on 90-day credit terms.

4b Sellers creates AR Payable in 90-days from delivery

Financier pays Sellers for purchased AR.

6a Sellers may sell AR to Financier according to pre-agreed AR Purchase Agreement.

6b

FINANCIER

BUYER

Buyer pays Financier each confirmed AR on its 90 day due date.

7

Buyer confirms to Financier it will pay Sellers' AR (Buyer's Trade Payables) on their 90-Day due dates.

5

1

Financier commits in SCF agreement with Buyer to purchase AR from (Buyer's Trade Payables) from Sellers that Buyer confirms it will pay on their extended 90-day due dates.

SCF Benefits and Considerations

Buyers

- Extended payment terms enable Buyers to better manage their working capital and cash flow needs, keeping in mind that Buyers need enough time for their purchased Items to generate revenue.

- Buyers can leverage their Trade Payables without having to take on additional secured loans or other collateralized debt, thereby avoiding disruption to their existing creditor relationships.

- Buyers can use SCF programs to strengthen their supply chain and Seller relationships, by making working capital more affordable to its Sellers that have less, or more costly, access to credit.

- Buyers retain control over their commercial relationships with their Sellers and will continue to decide which Trade Payables to pay in full or in part.

Sellers

- Sellers gain the opportunity to sell their AR to a Financier at interest rates based on the Buyer's creditworthiness, which in some cases may provide them with more cost-effective access to credit.

- Sellers have the option to grant extended payment terms but are not required to do so by the Buyer unless their Buyer makes participation in its SCF program a condition to doing business.

- Sellers will bear the cost of participating in a Buyer's SCF program, either by paying the Financier's interest rate if it sells its AR or, if it chooses not to sell its AR, by its additional working capital costs and payment risks it bears during the extended payment term.

- Sellers can purchase TCI to cover the Buyer's payment risk if it decides not to sell its AR during the extended payment term.

Financiers

- The Buyer's AR nonpayment risk can be covered by TCI.

- SCF programs can be a stable and growing source of recurring revenue, because they typically grow in size over time as more Sellers are on-boarded. Programs are often renewed annually as long as the Buyer risk remains stable and the program terms continue to make economic sense to the parties.

- SCF program administration and operations rely heavily on technology platforms that automate and streamline much of the day-to-day operations, thus making them more efficient than more manually operated TF transactions.

- SCF programs can be more efficient in terms of risk assessment and monitoring purposes, because only a single party's risks—the Buyer's—need to be assessed and monitored, rather than those of a group of diverse Buyers, which would be the case, for example, in a typical multi-Buyer AR Purchase Finance transaction. These benefits of having all Credit and other risks concentrated on a single Buyer also bring greater risk if the Buyer's creditworthiness declines, which can result in early program termination or catastrophic losses, depending on the program's size.

SCF Risk Mitigation

The most common way for SCF Financiers to mitigate the Buyer's nonpayment risk is to procure TCI with Indemnity Rates up to 95%, or 100% with a 5% first-loss Deductible. Most TC Insurers will cover SCF Buyer risks, despite their over-riding preference for covering diversified risks as well as their general aversion to covering large single Buyer risks. However, for SCF programs that involve large creditworthy Buyers with relatively short (e.g., 60 to 90 days) extended payment terms, the actual risk of Buyer nonpayment is considered to be relatively low. Nevertheless, many Financiers arranging such SCF transactions will still resort to using TCI to manage their internal Buyer Credit Risk limits. Using TCI may also improve a program's profitability if can be used to lower the amount of regulatory capital the Financier must keep on deposit for TF it extends. Obtaining regulatory capital relief, however, is dependent on constantly evolving bank accounting standards and how the specific TCI Contract is worded regarding any conditionality, certainty, and speed of potential claim payments.

Variations to SCF Programs

Syndicated SCF Programs

Large SCF programs, in terms of total dollar amounts at risk, are often syndicated or shared among several Financiers in order to address the arranging Financiers' single Buyer—or if TCI is used, single TC Insurer—Credit Risk limits. The syndication may be led by the Financier arranging the program or by an SCF technology platform provider that can both administer and arrange SCF programs but that generally does not fund transactions.

Turning Confirmed Payables into Negotiable Bills of Exchange

A Buyer may agree to transform its confirmed Trade Payables into Bills of Exchange issued by each Seller and accepted by the Buyer in order to make its Trade Payables more easily transferrable to a wider group of Financiers. A Buyer may agree to do this to reduce the Financiers' interest charges to its Sellers or, if its Trade volumes or nonpayment risks cannot be accommodated by a single Financier, to involve a greater number of Financiers. By accepting each Bill of Exchange, however, the Buyer waives any defenses to payment, including Trade Disputes or Dilution, against its Seller and any subsequent Holder of its Bill of Exchange. Nevertheless, the Buyer's Trade Payables that become Bills of Exchange can still remain classified as "trade debt" in its accounting records, rather than as a secured loan or bank debt.

Using Bill Of Exchange to Transform AR into Negotiable Debt Instrument

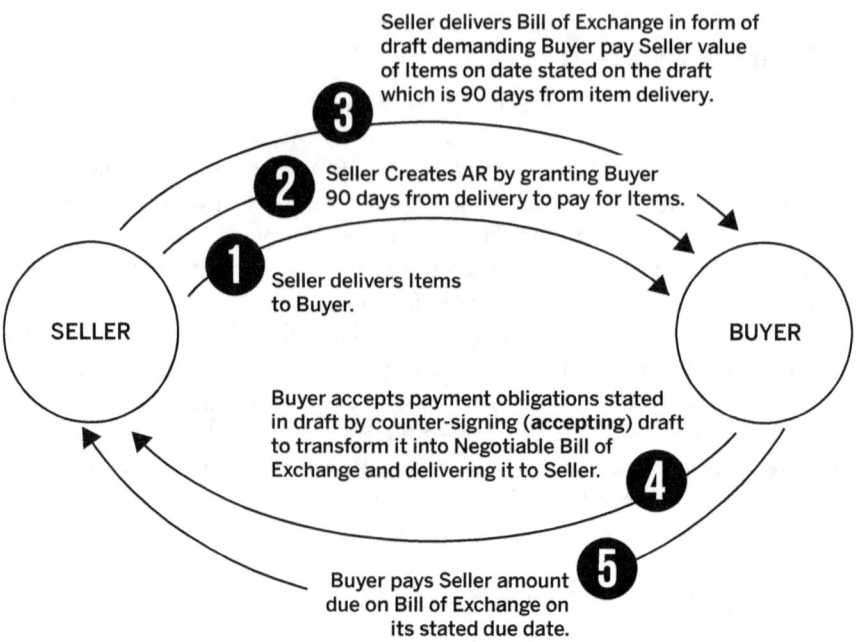

Seller delivers Bill of Exchange in form of draft demanding Buyer pay Seller value of Items on date stated on the draft which is 90 days from item delivery. **3**

Seller Creates AR by granting Buyer 90 days from delivery to pay for Items. **2**

1 Seller delivers Items to Buyer.

SELLER

BUYER

Buyer accepts payment obligations stated in draft by counter-signing (**accepting**) draft to transform it into Negotiable Bill of Exchange and delivering it to Seller. **4**

Buyer pays Seller amount due on Bill of Exchange on its stated due date. **5**

TCI OPTION: TCI may cover Seller against risk of Buyer failing to pay its Bill of Exchange due its financial inability.

DRAFT/BILL OF EXCHANGE

Issue Date: JANUARY 2, 2050

AMOUNT: $1,000,000
PAY ONE MILLION US DOLLARS
DRAWEE (Buyer): INTERNATIONAL IMPORTERS, DUBLIN, IRELAND

AGAINST PRESENTATION OF THIS SOLE BILL OF EXCHANGE
ON: APRIL 1, 2050 (Due Date)

TO DRAWER (Seller):
GLOBAL TRADERS INC., NEW YORK, AMERICAN UNITED BANK
ACCOUNT NUMBER 982101567

ACCEPTED: (Buyer/Drawee)
INTERNATIONAL IMPORTERS
DUBLIN IRELAND

DRAWER (Seller)
GLOBAL TRADERS INC.
NY, NY

_____
Buyer/Drawee's Signature

_____
Seller/Drawer's Signature

Supply Chain Finance Documentation

There are at least three essential contracts involved in SCF:

1) Each Trade agreement between the Buyer and its various Sellers covering the terms of each sale and the extended payment terms offered by the Sellers in exchange for its Financier agreeing to purchase the Seller's AR.

2) The Trade Payables Confirmation agreement between the Buyer and its Financier in which the Buyer agrees to confirm to the Financier its Trade Payables that it intends to pay on their respective due dates in exchange for the Financier agreeing to offer to purchase the corresponding AR from each Seller.

3) Each AR Purchase agreement entered into between the Financier and each participating on-boarded Seller stating the conditions and terms of each AR.

Other SCF agreements may include:

1) The Financier's TCI Contract.

2) A third-party SCF technology platform's agreement to administer the program.

3) Third-party service agreements for law firms, on-boarding companies, accountants, etc.

EARLY PAYMENT DISCOUNT FINANCE

Sellers that offer their Buyers Credit Terms may also offer a price discount if the Buyer pays for its Items earlier than the scheduled payment date. For example, under such an arrangement, if a Buyer's Trade Payable is due 30 days after Item delivery, but it pays early at delivery instead, the Seller will give the Buyer a price discount of about 1% to 2% flat of the Items' price, depending on the Seller's profit margins and working capital costs. If the Buyer wants to take advantage of this discount, but does not have the funds available to pay early or wants to preserve its available cash for other purposes, it may ask a Financier to step in and pay for the Items early on its behalf, if the Financier's Credit Terms make taking the Seller's discount worthwhile. In such cases, once the Financier pays the Seller early, the AR is extinguished, and the Financier then becomes a Lender to the Buyer, with the Buyer's debt to the Financier typically being documented in the form of a Loan Agreement or some other unconditional debt obligation with its Financier in which the Buyer waives any defenses to payment, including Trade Disputes or Dilution.

Early Payment Discounting makes economic sense for a Buyer if the Seller's discount rate compares favorably to the Buyer's short-term borrowing costs. For example, if a Seller offers its Buyer 30-day Credit Terms and an early payment discount of 2% flat of its Item's price of $1,000,000, the Buyer would save $20,000. The Seller's 30-day 2% flat early payment discount equates to a per annum interest rate savings of 24% (2% per month x 12 months). A 1% early payment discount rate equates to a per annum interest savings rate of 12%. Taking the 2% early payment discount would make economic sense for the Buyer if its Financier agrees to provide it funds ($980,000) at an interest rate below 24% p.a.

Seller Benefits

- Reduces Buyer nonpayment and other risks after having its AR paid early.

- Improves its working capital management by accelerating cash flow and sales recognition, while reducing days sales are outstanding (DSO), all of which can become especially important at a Seller's quarter end or other revenue reporting periods.

Buyer Benefits

- Lowers total cost of its Trades.

- Can use discount savings to subsidize working capital finance from Early Payment Financiers.

Financier Benefits

- Price discounts generate new source of funds to enable Buyers to affordably borrow short-term working capital.

- TCI is available to cover Buyer nonpayment risks, without risk of Trade Disputes or Dilution (because the original AR is extinguished at the time of early payment).

- Early Payment Discount Finance is not complex to market, execute, operate, or risk manage, thus making it a compelling and resource-efficient TF product for Financiers.

- Transactions are short-term, for single Buyer risks, and therefore relatively easy to assess and manage or to syndicate with other Financiers if needed.

Early Payment Discount Finance

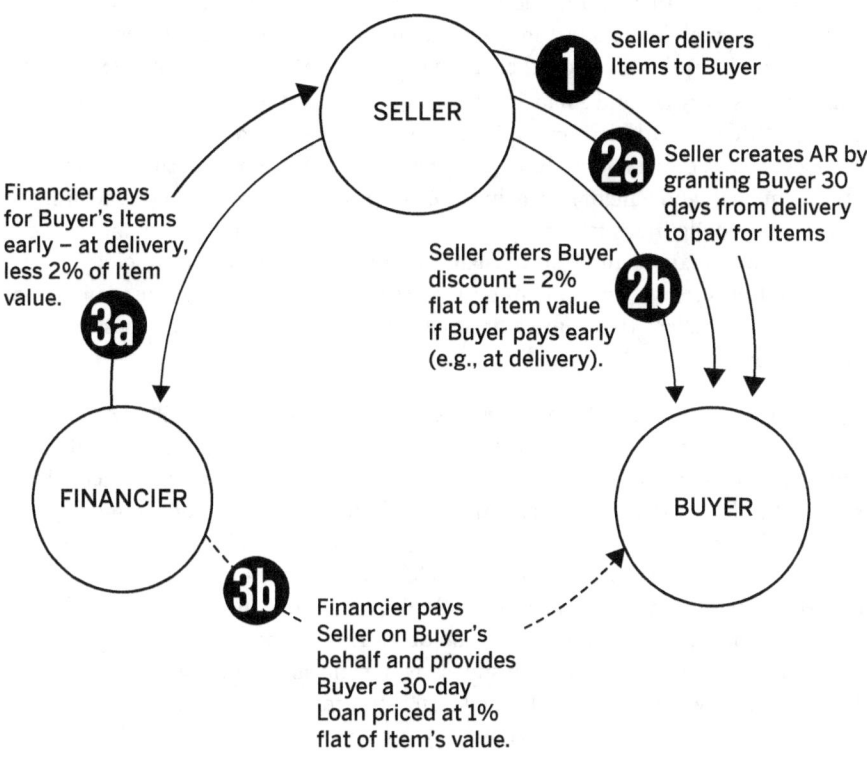

SELLER

1 Seller delivers Items to Buyer

2a Seller creates AR by granting Buyer 30 days from delivery to pay for Items

2b Seller offers Buyer discount = 2% flat of Item value if Buyer pays early (e.g., at delivery).

3a Financier pays for Buyer's Items early – at delivery, less 2% of Item value.

FINANCIER

3b Financier pays Seller on Buyer's behalf and provides Buyer a 30-day Loan priced at 1% flat of Item's value.

BUYER

TCI OPTION: TCI may cover Financier against risk of Buyer failing to repay Loan due its financial inability.

DISTRIBUTOR (AKA DEALER OR CHANNEL) FINANCE

Sellers often sell their Items to Buyers that are independent distributors or dealers (aka "channel partners," all referred to here as "Distributors"). The automobile and farm equipment industries provide good examples in which Sellers use a network of Distributors to market and sell their Items to the ultimate end-user Buyer. For example, automobile manufacturers sell automobiles to their independently owned dealers that keep the autos on their property and in their showrooms where they employ sales, service, and financing teams to help sell the autos to their ultimate Buyers. While these dealers are typically not owned by the manufacturer, they nevertheless enjoy special and exclusive commercial relationships that support one another's interests and which may include Distributor Financing. It is not uncommon in the automobile industry for dealers to receive 90-day or longer payment terms from the auto manufacturer or a Financier. Similarly, Sellers of technology infrastructure Items sell to independent businesses that install, integrate, customize, and transform the Seller's Items into a finished products for their own business or their ultimate Buyers.

Distributors can benefit from extended payment terms (e.g., 60, 90, 180 days or longer), when they need extra time to either market and sell their Items in their capacity as retailers or when they need to integrate or transform their Items into new and different Items for sale. If the Distributor requires Credit Terms beyond what its Seller can offer, a Financier may agree to step in and provide the Distributor with a loan or other form of Trade Debt that matures in 60, 90, or 180 days or more to bridge the gap. In this case, the Financier may pay the Seller, either at delivery or on the AR's original due date or some other date agreed to by the parties. Sellers have a significant interest in assisting and strengthening their profitable Distributor networks and will often take an active role in arranging, procuring, and even subsidizing, Distributor Finance programs.

Variations and Considerations

- Sellers may agree to pay all or part of a Distributor's financing costs charged by its Financier.

- Sellers may agree to provide a Distributor an initial Credit Period of 30 days or more before a Financier pays its AR and subsequently provides the Distributor with extended payment terms (e.g., the additional 60 or more days to pay), most typically in the form of loan.

- Distributors may want their extended payment terms to remain in the form of its original Trade Payable, rather than a loan, in order to avoid violating any loan covenants or other borrowing restrictions that may be in effect with its other Financiers. Alternatively, the Seller may want to maintain exclusive control over its relationship with its Distributor and avoid having a third-party Financier interact with its Distributor. In such cases, the Seller may agree to provide its Distributor with extended payment terms in the form of its original AR or a negotiable Bill of Exchange and then sell that AR to a Financier at any time of it choosing prior to its payment due date.

- TCI is available to cover the Distributor's nonpayment risk, whether its Trade Debt is in the form of an AR, Trade Payable, loan, or other form. Special attention needs to be paid to the TCI Contract to ensure that the insured is the ultimate owner of the Distributor's debt and possesses the requisite insurable interest.

Distribution, Dealer, Channel Finance

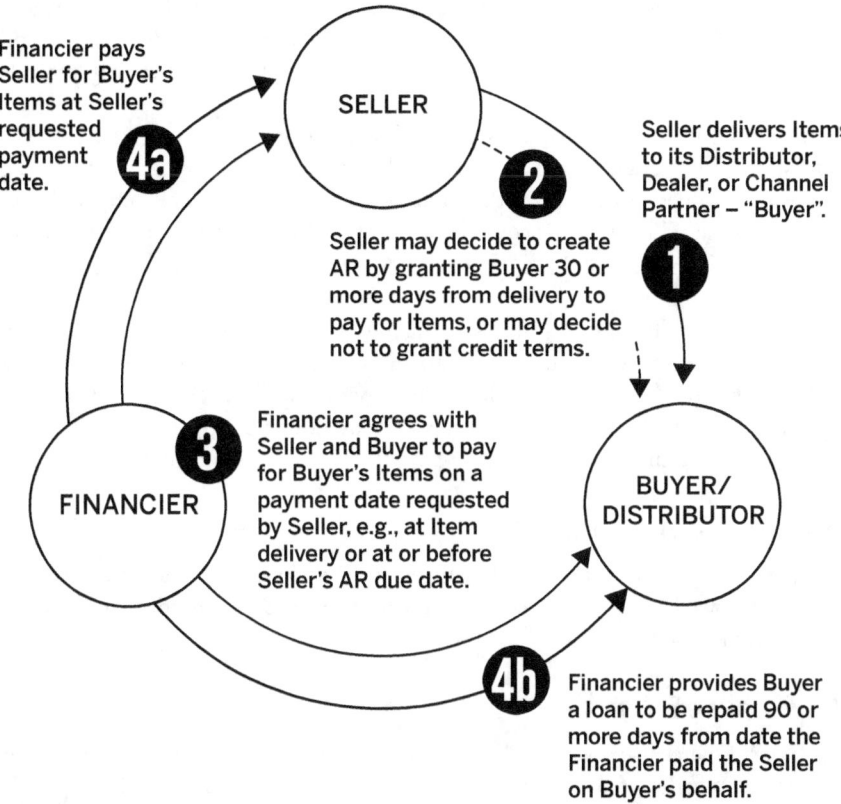

Financier pays Seller for Buyer's Items at Seller's requested payment date.
4a

SELLER

Seller delivers Items to its Distributor, Dealer, or Channel Partner – "Buyer".

2

1

Seller may decide to create AR by granting Buyer 30 or more days from delivery to pay for Items, or may decide not to grant credit terms.

3

FINANCIER

Financier agrees with Seller and Buyer to pay for Buyer's Items on a payment date requested by Seller, e.g., at Item delivery or at or before Seller's AR due date.

BUYER/ DISTRIBUTOR

4b Financier provides Buyer a loan to be repaid 90 or more days from date the Financier paid the Seller on Buyer's behalf.

TCI OPTION: TCI may cover Financier against risk of Buyer failing to repay Loan due its financial inability.

QUASI-TF SOLUTIONS

There are a number of highly specialized asset-based debt and other financing structures and solutions that are considered by many to be TF when they are used to support Trades in some manner. However, these so-called TF solutions are more accurately understood as variations of asset-based debt structures in which Credit and other risks are driven primarily by the Obligor's creditworthiness or the debt's collateral structure. Nevertheless, they are discussed briefly here because they may compete with, complement, or be confused with actual TF solutions.

Asset-Based Loans (ABLs)

Asset-Based Loans (ABLs) are a major source of working capital finance for businesses globally. ABLs are usually in the form of a one-year revolving Credit Facility, committed or not, in which the Obligor pledges all of its assets, including inventory, AR, cash, real estate, etc. to its Financier in exchange for the right to borrow and draw funds at its discretion to pay salaries, purchase inventory and materials, and cover operating costs and any other working capital needs. Financiers will typically file a legally recognized and recorded first-priority security interest (e.g., UCC security filing in the United States) over all of the Borrower's pledged assets. For Borrowers with moderate to low creditworthiness, their ABL Financiers' lending decisions will depend heavily on the value of the pledged loan collateral, or other loan security, and how easily it could be liquidated. These pledged loan assets form the Borrower's "borrowing base," which determines how much the Borrower may borrow from time to time. ABLs can, and often are, used by businesses in combination with the TF solutions discussed in this material. An ABL Financier may enhance the AR portion of its loan collateral by requiring the Borrower to procure TCI to cover its AR payment risk and by having the Financier named the loss payee in the TCI Contract, along with a separate power of attorney issued by the Borrower authorizing the Financier to execute TCI claims on its behalf.

Working Capital Loans

Working capital loans are an ABL whose stated purpose is for the Borrower to use the borrowed funds to procure, manufacture, or otherwise produce and deliver finished Items for Trade.

Pre-Export Finance

Pre-export finance usually takes the form of a loan or revolving Credit Facility that provides for a series of short-term Credit Advances made by a Financier, typically over the course of 12 months, to a Borrower that uses the funds to produce Items it plans to export. The Seller pledges its export proceeds (future export revenue) and, if needed, other collateral or security to the Financier to help secure the loan's repayment.

Purchase Order Finance

Purchase order finance typically takes the form of a loan or revolving Credit Facility that provides for a series of short-term Credit Advances made to a Seller by a Financier, typically over the course of 12 months, based on the expected future value of the Seller's purchase orders. When the purchase orders turn into actual Trades, the proceeds are used to repay the loan.

Financed Leasing

Financed Leases are best understood as loans legally disguised as leases to accomodate some special needs of the parties, typically for tax, accounting, or collateral risk mitigation or repossession purposes. A typical Financed Lease involves a Financier lending funds to a leasing company (a Lessor) that purchases Items that are subsequently leased to a Buyer (a Lessee). The Buyer/Lessee's lease payments to the Lessor serve to repay the Financier's loan to the Leasing company. For example, Financed Leasing is often used when financing the acquisition of moveable assets like planes or ships by foreign Buyers in cases where the Financier is not familiar with or lacks confidence in the legal system or the form of security it may receive over its collateral in a foreign country. Alternatively, a Buyer may have accounting, tax, or legal reasons for preferring a lease rather than a loan or other debt obligation. The leasing company to which the Financier lends funds may be an actual leasing business or a special purpose entity established specifically to support one or more Financed Leases.

Commodity Finance

Commodity Finance typically refers to an ABL or other form of secured debt created to support Trades or other transactions involving commodities (e.g., oil, foods, metals, etc.). Commodity Finance generally relies on the value of the commodities being Traded or otherwise pledged by some transaction party (e.g., Buyer or Seller) as debt collateral. While Commodity Finance often uses some other forms of TF (e.g., Letters of Credit, AR Finance, TCI, and ECAs) to help achieve its goals, it is better understood as a specialized secured debt product delivered by experts in commodities, rather than a form of TF.

Project Finance

Project Finance is a broad term covering various types of finance in the form of loans, equity investments, or other types of monetary, delivery, or performance commitments made by various parties to a project company. A Project Financier's Credit Risks are driven primarily by the project company's success in generating sufficient revenue to honor its financial or other obligations, or the creditworthiness of any guarantors or insurers on whose success the project company depends. For example, a Project Financier may have to rely not only on a project company building an electric generating power plant, but also on any utility companies that have guaranteed a minimum level of energy purchases according to agreed minimum price schedules. While Project Financiers may provide funds for a project company to procure Items and to pay for them over time, and may also use certain TF-related solutions, including Agency finance, Project Finance is, nevertheless, generally not considered to be TF.

Trading Company Finance

The use of trading companies in TF typically involves a Financier, through its Trading Company or one with which it partners, buying Items from a Seller and then reselling those Items to that Seller's original Buyer and then providing that Buyer with Credit Terms. A Financier can use this structure to mitigate or control several transaction risks in its Trade Debt to the Buyer, including Trade Dispute and Dilution, by being the first Buyer of the Items. A basic example of this structure is as follows:

- The Seller agrees to sell Items to its Buyer without Credit Terms.

- The Financier's Trading Company, with the Seller's and its Buyer's approval, buys the Items from the Seller for $1 mm, payable at delivery.

- The Trading Company sells the Items to the Buyer for $1,100,000, granting the Buyer 90-day Credit Terms documented as a negotiable Promissory Note in which the Buyer has waived any defense to payment.

Documentary Collections

Documentary Collections refers to a TF service (not actual financing) that banks provide to Sellers or Buyers to help them collect or pay amounts owed from their Trades. A bank will collect from the Seller any documents the Buyer requires as a condition to its payment, including any negotiable transport documents that would allow the Buyer to collect the Items from a carrier, and the Seller's Draft in which the Seller (as Drawer) orders payment from the Buyer (as Drawee). The collections bank will release the Seller's documents to the Buyer upon receipt of the Buyer's payment and will transfer the payment to the Seller, minus the bank's collections fee. The collections bank bears no responsibility to pay the Seller unless the Buyer makes its payment. The collections bank may agree to provide the Buyer with Credit Terms (e.g., 30, 60, 90 days) and will pay the Seller on its behalf. This alternative arrangement, however, will involve a separate Trade Debt agreement to be entered into between the collections bank and the Buyer.

CHAPTER 5

Funding TF Transactions

The manner in which a TF transaction is funded depends on its duration, structure, amount, and whether it utilizes a variable or fixed rate of interest. Fixed interest rates are generally reserved for one-off short-term debts and for some medium- and long-term TF transactions when their structure or market conditions make using them advantageous. Most other TF transactions, however, use a variable or "floating" interest rate. TF is typically funded in the currency in which the transaction is denominated, which means that a transaction denominated in USD will typically be funded in USD. Doing so avoids the risk of the funding currency fluctuating in value relative to a different transaction currency.

SELLER FUNDING ITS AR

When a Seller extends to its Buyers Credit Terms in the form of AR, it funds the transaction by putting at risk its own capital that it generates from its cash flow or by issuing debt. A Seller may decide to sell its AR if its cost of capital and risk exceeds the cost at which a Financier would purchase its AR.

FINANCIER FUNDING

A Financier's cost of funds is determined by its cost of borrowing funds from its depositors or other Financiers in the form of loans, bonds, commercial paper, or other debt issuances. A Financier funds a TF transaction by delivering funds directly to the Seller on behalf of its Buyer or other Obligor, usually at the time the Seller delivers its Items. A Financier may fund a transaction in full with a single Credit Advance corresponding to a Seller's single delivery or in a series of Credit Advances over time (e.g., 180 days) corresponding to each of the Seller's deliveries. For transactions with Credit Periods exceeding one year, multiple Credit Advances over a period a year or more are common.

Variable interest rates are determined by adding a Financier's fixed Margin to a published or otherwise accessible variable Interest Reference Rate that provides transparency and consistency. Financiers endeavor to use variable Interest Reference Rates that mirror as closely as possible their actual cost of funds. If a Financier's cost of funds exceeds the variable Interest Reference Rate being used in a transaction, it will need to increase its Margin accordingly to ensure that it earns a satisfactory return.

Bank Financiers traditionally funded TF transactions using funds borrowed from other banks in an interbank short-term lending market in order to "match fund" the exact amount with which it needed to fund each transaction. Today's larger Financiers, however, typically "pool fund" their TF and other transactions using funds raised through periodic borrowings or other general debt issuances. Non-bank Financiers may fund their transactions using standby credit lines extended by banks or other Financiers. A Financier's funding objective is to access funds reliably for the duration of its transaction, at the lowest possible cost, and to then pass its cost of funds as part of its total interest rate to its Obligor or to its Seller from which it purchases AR. A Financier's funding ability and its cost of funds depend primarily on its creditworthiness and on market conditions, both of which can change significantly over the duration of a transaction. An Obligor's or an AR Seller's funding objective is to select a Financier that has the funding capacity to reliably charge it the lowest possible total interest rate.

CAPITAL MARKET FUNDING

Another TF funding method involves a Financier issuing debt securities to capital market investors that are willing to sacrifice the level of liquidity they typically enjoy with bonds in exchange for the higher returns they can earn with a structured TF transaction. TF transactions funded in the capital markets are usually packaged into bond-like instruments, which requires a fair amount of costly, highly specialized structuring and legal work. For this reason, capital market funding is usually reserved for large dollar value transactions (e.g., $100 mm or more). These conditions make ECA-financed aircraft, shipping, or other large dollar transactions especially suited for capital market funding due to their size and the strong investor appetite for highly rated long-term government-guaranteed debt securities.

FUNDING USING VARIABLE INTEREST RATES

A Financier establishes its variable interest rate at the beginning of each Interest Period by adding its Margin to the agreed variable Interest Reference Rate, the latter of which is based on interest rate market conditions in effect on each funding date.

Variable Interest Reference Rates

A Financier's variable interest rate must be determined using a published or otherwise accessible variable Interest Reference Rate that provides transparency and consistency. Trade Debt denominated in US Dollars or Euros will typically be quoted using published US Dollar or Euro variable Interest Reference Rates, such as LIBOR or SOFR, the Euro Interbank Offered Rate (Euribor), the US Prime Rate, or other published rates that the parties can access on a regular basis for any given Interest Period. LIBOR and Euribor are established by taking the average interest rates at which large "prime" banks are willing to lend to each other in USD, Sterling (in the case of LIBOR), or Euros (in the case of Euribor) for maturities of 1 week to 1 year. Interest Referenced Rates should be available and quoted for one-month, three-month, and six-month Interest Periods. Bank Financiers have traditionally been the biggest users of LIBOR for their Interest Reference Rate. Non-bank TF Financiers may still use LIBOR as their Interest Reference Rate, depending on their size, credit rating, and borrowing ability. However, many non-bank TF Financiers raise their funds through standby credit facilities provided by their investors or banking partners or by selling all or part of their transactions to other Financiers. A Financier may agree with its Obligor to use an Interest Reference Rate that may be higher or lower than its actual cost of funds but which varies from it in a consistent range to allow its Margin to cover the anticipated gap in rates.

A Financier's actual cost of funds is likely to be higher or lower than LIBOR, depending on its creditworthiness. Accordingly, a Financier may adjust its Margin to accommodate the degree to which its cost of funds varies from its Interest Reference Rate. If, for example, a Financier intends to earn an interest Margin of at least 3% per annum, but its cost of funds consistently averages about 1% above its Interest Reference Rate, it may decide to charge its Obligor an interest rate of LIBOR plus 4% per annum.

LIBOR has been calculated by the Intercontinental Exchange (ICE) based on the interest rates offered by participating prime banks operating in the London market and posted by them by 11 a.m. (London time) on days on which banks are open in London. Euribor is calculated by the Trans-European Automated Real-Time Gross Settlement Express Transfer system based on the rates offered by prime banks operating in the Eurozone and posted by them by 11 a.m. Central European Time on days on which banks are open in the Eurozone. The Global Rate Set Systems (GRSS) publishes the reference rates to financial information providers (e.g., Bloomberg), which then make the rates available to their subscribers. LIBOR and Euribor rates are published two banking days prior to them becoming valid for interbank borrowing. For example, a Financier using LIBOR or Euribor to calculate its Interest Rates for an Interest Period beginning January 15 will use the LIBOR or Euribor rate that was published on January 13. This example assumes those are all days on which Eurozone or London banks are open. Otherwise, days on which banks are closed in those areas will be disregarded for counting the two prior days required for the rates to take effect. "Banking Days" with respect to determining LIBOR or Euribor or whatever Interest Reference Rate the parties select, will be defined in the parties' TF Agreement, typically as days on which the banks are authorized to open in London and in the countries in which the parties are located. Interest Reference Rates may vary from day to day depending on interest rate market movements and the number of days in a particular Interest Period.

The US Prime Rate is rarely used in international TF, though it can be found in some domestic TF transactions in the United States. The US Prime Rate is an average of short-term lending rates offered by the largest US banks and runs about 3% above the Federal Funds Rate, based on that rate's target set by the Federal Open Market Committee (FOMC) when they meet eight times a year.

LIBOR To Be Phased Out by 2023

As of the date of this writing, after 2021, banks will not be compelled by their respective regulators to submit their periodic LIBOR borrowing rates, which is expected to result in the phaseout of LIBOR by the end of 2023. Banks and regulators are now in the process of establishing alternative reference rates. One alternative rate being considered is the Secured Overnight Financing Rate (SOFR), which is a broad measure of the cost of borrowing cash overnight relatively risk free and collateralized by US Treasury securities. SOFR is published daily by the Federal Reserve Bank of New York. Being an overnight rate, rather than a forward-looking short-term rate like LIBOR, a Financier's accompanying Margin over SOFR will need to include its prediction of its cost of funds during each Interest Period. In any case, Financiers using LIBOR need to be prepared for its phaseout and include an alternative reference rate mechanism in any TF transaction with Credit Periods extending beyond 2023.

Variable Interest Rate Funding

A Financier that uses SOFR, or any other Interest Reference Rate will establish its total interest rate to its Obligor at the beginning of each Interest Period. For example, consider a $4 mm loan that is repayable in 4 equal ($1 mm) semi-annual principal payments over a 2-year Credit Period that has 4 six-month Interest Periods and an interest rate quoted as "6-month Interest Reference Rate plus its Margin of 3% p.a." At the beginning of the first six-month Interest Period, the Financier will borrow $4 mm from its Interest Reference Rate Financier based on the published six-month Interest Reference Rate in effect, according to market protocol, two business days prior to its actual funding date, which for this example will be 1% p.a. At the end of the first 6-month Interest Period, the Obligor repays the Financier $1mm in principal plus interest at 4% p.a. on $4 mm for six months ($80,000). The Financier uses the Obligor's first principal payment to pay its Interest Reference Rate Financier $1 mm plus interest on $4 mm at 1% p.a. for 6 months ($20,000), thus allowing the Financier to earn its Margin of $60,000. The Financier repays its Interest Reference Rate Financier the remaining $3 mm it owes it from funds the Financier borrows for the next six-month Interest Period from that or another Interest Reference Rate Financier. If for any reason the Financier is forced to repay a Interest Reference Rate Financier any principal prior to the end of any 6-month Interest Period, the Obligor and its Financier will be required to pay the Interest Reference Rate Financier additional "interest rate breakage" costs if the Interest Reference Rate Financier will lose money due to the early principal repayment. Interest breakage costs may be triggered due to early voluntary or involuntary payment of a Trade Debt, or a Guarantor's or TC Insurer's early payment to the Financier in case the Obligor is unable to pay. Guarantors and TC Insurers generally retain the right to honor their payment obligations on days they determine are consistent with their Guarantee or TCI Contracts, rather than the Financier's amortization or Interest Reference Rate interbank borrowing schedules. Accordingly, interest breakage costs are a Financier's funding risk that needs to be taken into account when structuring a TF transaction.

If a Financier funds a transaction using a series of Credit Advances, it will establish a variable interest rate for each Credit Advance. For example, in our 2-year, $4 mm loan example above, if the Credit Facility Validity Period is 180 days, two Credit Advances will be made during that period to correspond to two Seller deliveries valued at $2 mm each. The first $2 mm Credit Advance is made 150 days before the end of the Credit Facility Validity Period, for which the Financier establishes its first variable interest rate applicable to $2 mm for a 150-day Interest Period. The second $2 mm Credit Advance is made 90 days before the end of the Credit Facility Validity Period, for which the Financier establishes its second variable interest rate applicable to $2 mm for a 90-day Interest Period. At the end of the Credit Facility Validity Period, the Financier will establish a single variable interest rate applicable to the entire $4 mm for the first of four 180-day Interest Periods.

Funding Trade Debt With Variable Interest Rate

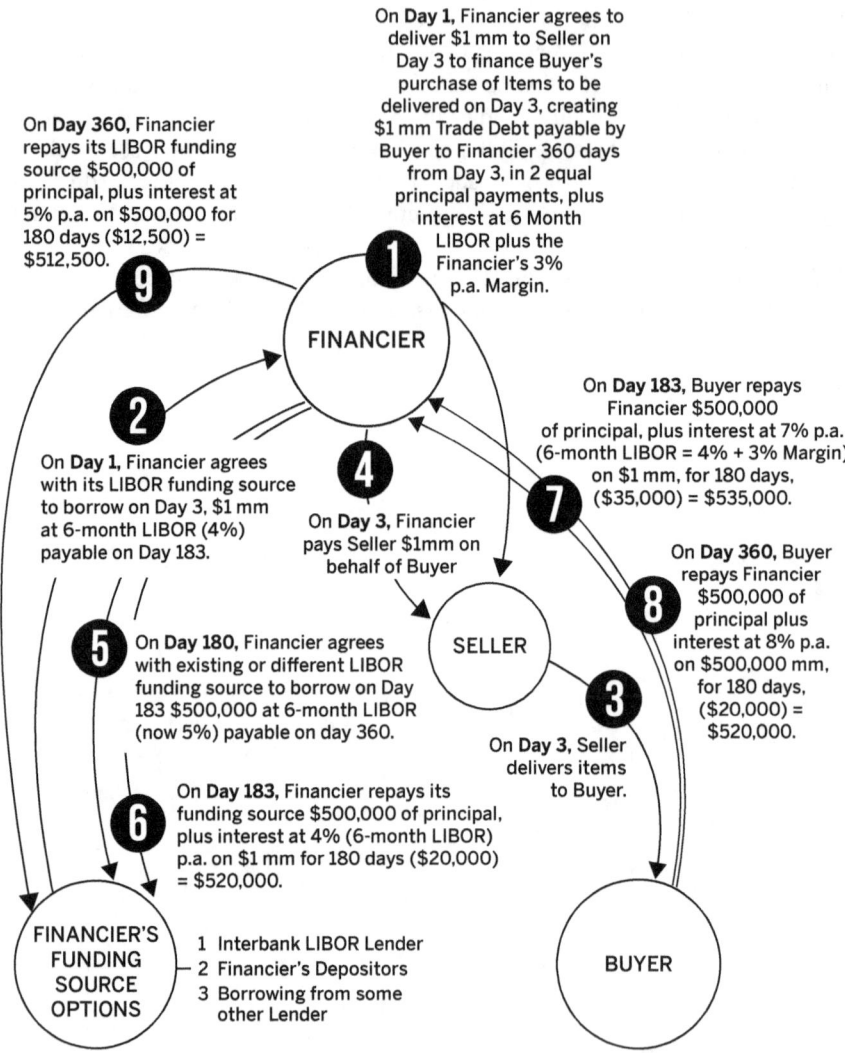

On **Day 1,** Financier agrees to deliver $1 mm to Seller on Day 3 to finance Buyer's purchase of Items to be delivered on Day 3, creating $1 mm Trade Debt payable by Buyer to Financier 360 days from Day 3, in 2 equal principal payments, plus interest at 6 Month LIBOR plus the Financier's 3% p.a. Margin.

①

On **Day 360,** Financier repays its LIBOR funding source $500,000 of principal, plus interest at 5% p.a. on $500,000 for 180 days ($12,500) = $512,500.

⑨

FINANCIER

②

On **Day 1,** Financier agrees with its LIBOR funding source to borrow on Day 3, $1 mm at 6-month LIBOR (4%) payable on Day 183.

④

On **Day 3,** Financier pays Seller $1mm on behalf of Buyer

On **Day 183,** Buyer repays Financier $500,000 of principal, plus interest at 7% p.a. (6-month LIBOR = 4% + 3% Margin) on $1 mm, for 180 days, ($35,000) = $535,000.

⑦

On **Day 360,** Buyer repays Financier $500,000 of principal plus interest at 8% p.a. on $500,000 mm, for 180 days, ($20,000) = $520,000.

⑧

SELLER

⑤ On **Day 180,** Financier agrees with existing or different LIBOR funding source to borrow on Day 183 $500,000 at 6-month LIBOR (now 5%) payable on day 360.

③

On **Day 3,** Seller delivers items to Buyer.

⑥ On **Day 183,** Financier repays its funding source $500,000 of principal, plus interest at 4% (6-month LIBOR) p.a. on $1 mm for 180 days ($20,000) = $520,000.

FINANCIER'S FUNDING SOURCE OPTIONS

1 Interbank LIBOR Lender
2 Financier's Depositors
3 Borrowing from some other Lender

BUYER

FIXED INTEREST RATES – SWAPS, CAPS

Funding TF Using Fixed Interest Rates

Fixed-rate funding is more complicated than funding using variable interest rates; therefore, fixed interest rates are used for a very small percentage of TF transactions globally, other than Seller-financed short-term AR or some medium- or long-term transactions. Fixed interest rates are also used for Financed Lease transactions commonly used for long-term ship, large equipment, or aircraft financings for which the exact amounts of all future principal and interest payments coming due during the life of the transaction need to be known in advance in order to structure them as a series of equal "rental" payment amounts.

Fixed Rate Borrowing

One way a Financier could provide a fixed interest rate is by borrowing funds at a fixed cost for the duration of the Trade Debt's Credit Period. Funding a fixed interest rate in this manner requires the Financier and its Obligor to commit in advance to an exact repayment schedule for the Trade Debt's principal and interest. If there is any deviation of this schedule or amounts, including any payment shortfalls or early principal pre-payments, interest breakage costs will result if the Financier's fixed-rate provider loses money when redeploying the funds. For example, a Financier needs to fund its $4 mm loan that is repayable in 4 equal semi-annual principal payments over a 2-year Credit Period, resulting in 4 six-month Interest Periods. The Financier intends to earn a Margin of 1% p.a. from its Obligor, and quotes it a fixed interest rate of 4% p.a. The Financier will need to fund $4 mm by borrowing it from some other Financier at a fixed rate of 3% p.a.

Interest Rate Swaps

A Financier could also provide a fixed interest rate by entering into an Interest Rate Swap agreement with another Financier (its Swap Counterparty) that specializes in providing interest rate derivatives, in which it exchanges (swaps) its Obligor's fixed interest payments (less its Margin) for short-term interest payments to cover its short-term funding costs. For example, using our $4 mm Trade Debt example above, the Financier would charge its Obligor a fixed interest rate of 4% p.a. and will borrow funds for each Interest Period in the variable interbank market at 6-month Interest Reference Rate. On each semi-annual interest payment date, the Financier will swap its Obligor's fixed interest payments of 3% p.a. (4% less the 1% Margin) to its Swap Counterparty in exchange for the Swap Counterparty delivering to the Financier interest payments at a rate of 6-month Interest Reference Rate. In this example, the Swap Counterparty is earning a *swap rate* of 3% p.a. from the Financier.

The Swap Counterparty determines its swap rate by predicting what the swapped variable interest rates (6-month Interest Reference Rate in this example) are likely to be throughout a Trade Debt's Credit Period based on the current price of bonds and other debt instruments of similar duration and creditworthiness. Both the Financier and the Swap Counterparty will be taking each other's Credit Risk during the Trade Debt's Credit Period. If the Financier needs to break or "unwind" its Swap agreement due to its Obligor's payment default or early payment of the Trade Debt, the Financier will need to pay its Swap Counterparty breakage costs for any losses it would incur for redeploying its funds to recoup its expected revenue for the entire life of the Swap agreement.

Interest Rate Caps

Another way to provide a fixed or maximum interest rate is by having either the Financier or its Obligor purchase an interest rate Cap from a Financier that specializes in providing interest rate derivatives. An interest rate Cap allows a Financier's cost of funds or an Obligor's interest rate to be capped to go no higher than an agreed rate (Cap Strike Price). For example, the Financier is funding a $4 mm Trade Debt that amortizes over 2 years in 4 equal semi-annual principal payments, and four 6-month Interest Periods. It is charging its Obligor a variable interest rate of 6-month Interest Reference Rate plus 3% p.a. and wants to limit its cost of 6-month Interest Reference Rate to no more than 1% p.a. over the 2 years, so it purchases a 2-year, 6-month Interest Reference Rate Cap with a Strike Price of 1% p.a. If the six-month Interest Reference Rate ever exceeds 1% p.a. on the day of any interest rate setting date the Cap Counterparty will pay the Financier interest for that Interest Period at the rate the six-month Interest Reference Rate exceeds 1% p.a. The Obligor may also independently purchase its own interest rate Cap directly from a Financier/Swap Counterparty to Cap its maximum interest rate. Interest rate Caps are not limited to Interest Reference Rate prices but may also be purchased to apply to other published Interest Reference Rates. Caps will vary in price depending on how wide the difference is between the agreed Strike Price and current Interest Reference Rates. The wider the difference, the lower the Cap's cost. For example, if the 6-month Interest Reference Rate is currently 1% p.a., purchasing an Interest Reference Rate Cap with a Strike Price of 6% p.a. for a Trade Debt amortizing over 2 years would be relatively inexpensive compared to a Cap with a Strike Price of 2% p.a. Since Cap costs are known and payable up front, the Swap Counterparty bears no Counterparty Credit Risks, unlike with an Interest Rate Swap in which both parties rely on the other to deliver funds over time. Another benefit to using a Cap is that its cost may be added to the total amount of Trade Debt and financed (capitalized) over time, and because the Cap Counterparty receives all its revenue up front, there can be no breakage costs if the Obligor defaults or repays the Trade Debt early. Despite these potential advantages, interest rate Caps are not commonly used in TF, most likely due to the prevailing custom and practice of using variable interest rates, and perhaps because interest rates in general have been relatively low and stable since the 2008 financial crisis.

Fixed Interest Rate Loan Assignments or Participations

A TF Financier may provide its Obligor a fixed interest rate by selling its Trade Debt, by means of Assignment or Participation, to another Financier that prefers holding fixed interest rate assets that are typically structured as bonds or long-term loans.

Export Credit Agencies Fixed Rates

Many ECAs offer Financiers and Obligors the ability to borrow at fixed interest rates. Some ECAs, such as US EXIM, provide fixed interest rate loans directly to Obligors, using the official fixed interest lending rates, called the Commercial Interest Reference Rates (CIRR), agreed among the Export Credit Agencies. CIRR is calculated monthly based on government bonds issued in the country's domestic market for that ECA's currency. In the case of the US Dollar, the CIRR is based on the US Treasury bond rate. US EXIM also enables its Guaranteed Lenders to provide fixed interest rates with little or no risk of swap or other breakage costs by agreeing to pay any fixed interest rate loan Guarantee claims according to the guaranteed loan's original amortization schedule, thus avoiding any need to unwind any fixed Interest Rate Swap the Financier may have entered into. Some other ECAs, mainly in Europe, agree to subsidize a Financier's ECA-insured fixed interest rate loans through an interest make-up agreement, in which the Financier funds a fixed interest rate loan to a Borrower with a variable interest rate, and the ECA guarantees the Financier a certain level of interest so that it does not lose money through its funding.

CHAPTER 6

Compliance and Know Your Customer (KYC)

Each party to a TF transaction, especially deep-pocket Financiers and other arranging parties, should diligently examine and review their transactions and the involved parties to ensure they do not violate applicable laws, regulations (external compliance), or their internal rules (internal compliance). Each transaction party will need to follow its own compliance and "know your customer" (KYC) process in order to protect itself against potential liability that may arise from doing business with parties with which they are prohibited by law from doing so or those potentially engaged in money laundering or other illegal activities. KYC and compliance procedures are good not only for developing healthy business relationships, but also for avoiding or revealing fraudulent activity by customers or employees. Unfortunately, the efforts and resources many businesses dedicate to compliance and KYC are often minimal or nonexistent and, in many cases, focused only on Credit Risks, as opposed to fraud or compliance risks. Nevertheless, it is an essential and good business practice for any TF transaction party to know its customers and counterparties, their creditworthiness (e.g., can Buyers pay their bills, will Sellers honor their warranties?), business growth plans and prospects (will the party be a good long-term partner?), with whom and where they do business, and other factors that are relevant to a healthy, appropriately transparent business relationship.

Most government regulators require banks, TC Insurers, and certain other businesses to adopt and follow fairly robust KYC procedures to meet the regulators' minimum requirements for compliance or face the prospect of fines or loss of license. Unregulated businesses adopt and follow their own KYC procedures to varying degrees of intensity. For banks, the key KYC requirements include reviewing documents that evidence the identity of their customer's owners (e.g., the majority shareholders' identities), their customer's financial statements, the nature and location of its business activities, and whether their customer or its owners appear on any government-issued sanctions list that prohibits doing business with them. The United States issues sanctions lists through its Office of Foreign Assets Control (OFAC), an office of the US Department of the Treasury that administers and enforces economic and trade sanctions, based on US foreign policy and national security goals, against targeted foreign countries and regimes, terrorists, international narcotics traffickers, those engaged in activities related to the proliferation of weapons of mass destruction, and other threats to the national security, foreign policy, or economy of the United States. Regulated businesses in the US and regulated foreign companies doing business in the US are required to screen their customers against OFAC-administered sanctions lists. If there is a match, the business is required to ascertain if the match is genuine or simply another person or business with the same name as the entity on the sanctions list. If the match is genuine, the business must block the transaction and report its findings to OFAC. If the match is not genuine, the business may continue with the transaction. It is important to note that unregulated businesses in the US are also prohibited from doing business with businesses on the sanctions list and therefore should include a sanctions check in their KYC procedures.

Some government regulators require regulated businesses to determine the identity of their customer's ultimate beneficial owner (UBO) and to screen them against government-issued sanctioned lists. Unless a customer identifies its UBO(s) voluntarily, it is difficult for any third party to identify the actual UBO(s), since that information is normally not publicly available. For example, it is relatively easy in several countries, including in some US States, to create a shell company for which the UBO is not registered or made public. Some countries and local jurisdictions in which businesses establish legal existence (e.g., through incorporation), do publish a registry identifying owners of their registered businesses, but they do not necessarily identify the UBOs in cases where the UBO nominates another person or business to appear as the registered owner (or nominee). Moreover, people and businesses who are on a government-issued sanctions list generally take measures to hide their ownership or involvement in their business transactions and will not be in the practice of either voluntarily disclosing their identity or allowing it to appear in any public records or financial statements.

Banks, TC Insurers, and other regulated TF parties are also required by law in the US and most other developed money-center countries to examine their customers' behaviors and their proposed transactions to identify any potential compliance issues or suspicious behaviors, or other factors that may require additional investigation, before engaging or continuing business with that entity. While TF fraud is perceived by many to occur mainly in transactions with developing countries, it should be noted that the developed exporting countries are among the largest participants in foreign bribery. According to Transparency International's 2018 edition of its Exporting Corruption Report, over half of global exports come from countries that fail to punish foreign bribery.[16]

In addition to being used to facilitate bribery, TF can be used to facilitate money laundering. This may be done by creating fictitious unperformed Trades with an accomplice Buyer in which a Buyer makes a payment to the Seller without any

---

16   Transparency International, "Export Corruption Report", September 12, 2018, https://www.transparency.org/en/press/over-half-of-global-exports-come-from-countries-that-fail-to-punish-foreign

goods or services being exchanged. Another way to launder money is for a Seller to inflate the price of goods for an actual Trade with an accomplice Buyer in order to justify a larger than normal payment from the Buyer, the excess of which becomes laundered money. For example, a Seller would sell $1 mm of used autos, loose cut diamonds, or works of art to an accomplice Buyer for a price of $2 mm in order to launder the $1 mm of "profit." There are numerous other ways to commit fraud and launder money using TF. The US government's interagency body, the Federal Financial Institutions Examination Council (FFIEC) publishes a comprehensive list of money laundering "red flags."[17] The following are additional behaviors or factors that may indicate the presence of fraud, money laundering, or other illegal activity in connection with TF transactions:

- The use of local agents, sometimes referred to as consultants, facilitation agents, or advisors, that are well connected to government or other high-level decision makers in a Buyer's country. These local agents help Sellers arrange meetings with potential Buyers and provide advice on how to win and execute business. While these agents often play useful, legitimate roles, they may also be used to funnel bribes to the Buyer, the funds for which may be generated with inflated sales commissions that the Seller pays to the local agent. Many large, well-known international businesses have been accused or convicted of bribery done in this manner.[18] These local agents are often independent contractors employed by the Seller and generally do not appear in transaction documents, unless they insist on being named in order to build their business reputation or to help legitimize their presence in a transaction.

- Inflated, uncompetitive contract prices, usually associated with sole-sourced contracts where no open bidding process was followed. The inflated prices are a sign that extra profits need to be generated to pay for bribes to various parties, including local agents, port or transportation authorities, or other parties with the power to approve or block all or part of a transaction.

---

17   Federal Financial Institutions Examination Council, "BSA/AML Manual: Appendix F: Money Laundering and Terrorist Financing 'Red Flags'", https://bsaaml.ffiec.gov/manual/Appendices/07

18   Transparency International, "CPI 2020: Trouble at the Top - An Analysis", January 28, 2021, https://www.transparency.org/en/news/cpi-2020-trouble-at-the-top.

CHAPTER 7

TF FinTech and e-Commerce

FinTech and innovative e-Commerce services and solutions are providing new ways to conduct TF by leveraging new technologies, including artificial intelligence (AI), the internet of things (IoT), and blockchain and distributed ledgers. FinTech is heavily focused on digitizing and automating transaction origination, execution, and administration, and creating online platforms and marketplaces to connect TF market participants.[19] Discussed below are some of the various FinTech and e-Commerce technologies and solutions in use or being developed for TF.

DIGITIZATION

Digitizing communications, documents, assets, title documents, and other transaction records is a precondition to virtually all meaningful FinTech solutions and innovations. Digitization of actionable data requires the use of *structured data* that can be transmitted, interpreted, and acted upon by the communicating technologies. Businesses that intend to benefit from FinTech therefore need to digitize their relevant current and past data into structured data that can be organized, enriched, analyzed, reconfigured, and securely stored for easy access and future sharing with counterparties. Electronic data interchange (EDI) is the technology that enables structured data to be exchanged and interpreted among transaction parties' computers and other data systems. For example, transmitting an invoice in a non-structured data format like PDF does not enable the recipient's technology to automatically interpret and act intelligently on that invoice's data. The recipient of a PDF invoice would need to manually review and validate the invoice, and then manually initiate a payment to the sender. Alternatively, the recipient could use optical character recognition (OCR) software to convert the PDF information into structured data. OCR software, however, cannot reliably convert the data with 100% accuracy

---

19 The International Chamber of Commerce (ICC)'s 2018 Global Survey reports that over 60% of banks surveyed have implemented or are in process of implementing technology solutions to digitalize their trade finance operations. Only 9% of banks reported that the solutions implemented have so far led to a reduction of time and costs in trade finance transactions. The report concludes that the industry needs more common standards so that all the benefits of trade digitalisation can be realized. https://iccwbo.org/publication/global-survey-2018-securing-future-growth/

and adds a cumbersome, inefficient layer of intermediary technology that is better used to bridge the gap between legacy and modern systems that have no choice but to continue communicating using both unstructured and structured data.

ARTIFICIAL INTELLIGENCE (AI)

AI uses software to simulate human intelligence and capabilities to improve TF data analytics, credit analysis, and business origination and retention. AI can analyze large amounts of data quickly to assess numerous scenarios and forecast probable outcomes to guide its users' decision making. AI-based tools are being developed for TF to help automate, speed, and improve credit analysis and credit exposure decision making for Buyers, Sellers, and Borrowers. AI advancements promise, among many other things, to:

- Reduce or eliminate the majority of manual Credit Risk underwriting processes in the banking and TCI industry.

- Perform credit analysis that, in addition to traditional credit assessment data and tools, includes non-traditional data, credit patterns, and credit-relevant business behaviors.

- Improve transaction pricing by analyzing and learning from current and past transactions, and comparing available market benchmarks and trends.

- Originate new business by matching suitable counterparties according to their needs (Buyers, Sellers, Financiers, Insurers, etc.).

- Help retain existing business through improved client focus and service by analyzing client data and behavior to identify client behaviors or communications that may reveal low or high customer service satisfaction.

- Detect fraud by analyzing transaction patterns and alerting relevant parties or regulators to potential fraudulent or suspicious behavior.

INTERNET OF THINGS (IOT)

IoT involves physical objects (goods, shipping containers, trucks, livestock, etc.) being installed with devices that can sense, analyze, and transmit actionable data over the internet to an interested party. Data from these connected objects can be used for various purposes such as tracking the temperature of cargo containers shipping wine across the ocean and locating a cargo's location in transit. For TF, the focus of IoT is mainly on tracking or monitoring the origin, location, or condition of goods from their production to delivery, from Seller to Buyer, or among other transaction participants, whether by ocean, road, or air. Tracking the movement and real-time location of goods, especially perishables, can be used to monitor or verify their condition or quality, to trigger the legal transfer of goods, or to initiate payment to the Seller or other parties. IoT can also be applied to Trades of agricultural or other commodities for which information about an Item's origin or condition can be important for various health and consumer transparency issues.

BLOCKCHAIN

Blockchain, in currently popular cryptocurrency form, involves using decentralized databases that communicate among common users through their specially configured computer systems called "nodes" to validate and record the exchange of value (e.g., cryptocurrency) among anonymous users. Most cryptocurrency transaction are validated by third parties using complex computer programming and problem solving (e.g., "miners" for Bitcoin) or some other consensus method that makes it difficult or impossible to double create or double spend the cryptocurrency. Blockchain is used to create unique forms of value, including tokens, currencies, or other digital objects. It does this by transforming the state of a set of digital information or representations into a new unique state and form of value. For example, Blockchain can transform the state of two parties' exchanged financial data into a new, unique, verifiable cryptocurrency transaction. However, for Blockchain to be useful for finance, including TF, a non-anonymous system for exchanging value is evolving, called distributed ledger technology (DLT). The term "ledger" means a firm's list of assets, and "distributed" means sharing data about those assets with one or more permissioned transaction counterparties in order for them to exchange value or to conclude a transaction. Unlike Blockchain for cryptocurrency, DLT allows access to the shared data to only those parties that have an approved need. Basically, this means two or more contracting parties could use DLT to share, only among themselves, the data needed to execute a transaction. Using DLT, instead of current manual transaction execution practices, is intended to achieve one or more of the following benefits: (a) generally lowering transaction costs and increasing efficiency through the use of digitized and automated transacting; (b) speeding transaction execution by reducing the number of steps needed to validate and execute it; (c) reducing transaction errors; (d) increasing transaction transparency from start to finish by recording each step of a transaction; (e) enhancing transaction integrity and security by increasing the difficulty of unauthorized alteration or amendment of transaction data; and (f) promoting connectivity and ease of collaboration among parties through the use of a common platform, or by using common protocols that are interoperable among different data systems and transaction platforms.

In its most basic form, DLT enables contracting parties to record their transactions on a DLT platform that provides pre-agreed levels of visibility to each party. A more complex use of DLT involves the parties actually executing their financial transaction using a DLT platform. To execute financial transactions, the parties need to use legally binding digital contracts that can self-execute themselves based on each party's or other third-parties' inputs. These digital self-executing contracts are sometimes referred to as "smart contracts." For example, if a Seller delivers goods to the Buyer and the party's smart contract is notified of this delivery and that other smart-contract conditions were satisfied, funds could automatically be released to the Seller. Keep in mind the smart contract's notice of satisfactory delivery may need to come from the Buyer after it inspects the goods, despite the fact that the objective of using smart contracts is to automate as much of the transaction as possible. Additionally, DLT platforms and DLT-executed smart contracts are designed to accept data from other external trusted sources, some of which are referred to as "oracles," that can provide pricing, location services, or other relevant data to the smart contract or other parties. That data may be used to satisfy or trigger a contractual condition among interested parties. For example, a Buyer may agree in its smart contract to have its payment released automatically to the Seller once the Seller's Items arrive at the Buyer's port. An oracle or other trusted data source could inform the smart contract when the ship carrying the Items arrives at the Buyer's port, which could trigger the Buyer's payment. Before any user can benefit from using DLT to transact or interact with counterparties, Buyers, Sellers, shippers, auditors, regulators, etc. using smart contracts or other means, it will first need to digitize its relevant data in a format that can be accessed and shared externally using DLT.

ONLINE TRANSACTIONAL MARKET PLACES

Online Market Places are web-based platforms in which Sellers, Buyers, TC Insurers, Brokers, Financiers, and other TF market participants are intended to connect, collaborate, arrange, structure, and execute TF transactions more efficiently than with traditional methods. Market Places have the potential to offer a wide variety of competitive financial products and services from many types of providers, giving their users the best chances of connecting and doing business with the most suitable counterparties. To be effective, though, Market Places need to achieve a critical mass of both customers and service providers. Some Market Places specialize in providing only one or a very limited number of TF services (e.g., only Confirmed Payables, or only AR Purchase). Other Market Places may focus on providing TF to small- and medium-size businesses, for which there is perceived to be a large underserved and potentially lucrative TF market.

ONLINE MARKETING AND SALES PORTALS

Online portals operate simply as web-based sales tools that provide their users the ability to learn about and submit applications online for TF or TF services such as TCI but which are then followed up with manual and traditional processes to provide the requested TF product or service. These sales portals' objective is to reach a broad group of prospective clients by offering them an easy online information source and application process. They are usually operated by a single Financier, TC Insurer, or other TF service provider.

AR PURCHASE FINANCE APPLICATIONS

Some Online Market Places provide their users specific applications to facilitate AR Purchase Finance. AR Sellers can use these systems to select the AR they want to sell, based on amount, maturity, and Buyer creditworthiness, to achieve optimal working capital management, and to then offer that AR for sale to interested Financiers. Financiers can use these systems to execute their AR Purchases, automating most of the process for AR presentation, validation, payment, and collections. Because these systems may be integrated into a Seller's accounting system, they may be capable of producing credit and other valuable financial reports that evaluate each AR's Credit Risk and payment performance. This real-time transaction data would be valuable to potential Financiers and other TF providers for making informed decisions quickly, and could help the Seller achieve the best possible AR Purchase Finance outcomes.

SUPPLY CHAIN FINANCE/CONFIRMED PAYABLES PLATFORMS

SCF platforms which have already been in use for over 20 years enable SCF program participants to do the following on a fully or semi-automated basis, depending on the level of platform sophistication: (a) Buyers to confirm their payables to their Financier(s); (b) Financiers to offer to purchase Sellers AR corresponding to Confirmed Payables; (c) Sellers to execute their sale of AR to the Financiers; and (d) Financiers to reconcile the Buyer's payments to the AR they purchase. Some SCF platforms help facilitate the Financier's "on-boarding" of participating Sellers to the platform. On-boarding means authorizing, registering, and training each Seller for use of the Platform as well as conducting a KYC process for each Seller.

PROCURE TO PAY APPLICATIONS

The terms Procure to Pay describes a Buyer's process of purchasing an Item, beginning with a Buyer's purchase order, Item review and acceptance, payment execution, and financing if required. A great deal of existing technology is involved in automating and streamlining the Procure to Pay process. Procure to Pay TF solutions are often provided by specialized technology businesses working in cooperation or partnership with Financiers.

INSURETECH

InsureTech refers generally to the use of existing and emerging technologies to improve the quality, efficiency, and delivery of TCI and other Insurance products and services by digitizing and automating an Insurer's end-to-end processes, including new business development, underwriting, Contract execution, policy administration, and claims management. TC Insurers, for example, may introduce online applications that can interpret the applicant's needs and, within minutes instead of days, deliver a quote. Other services are emerging that feed TCI applications to multiple Insurers or Brokers in order to obtain competitive quotes.

TCI UNDERWRITING APPLICATIONS

The current state of TCI underwriting involves a great deal of subjective and manual Credit decision making, requiring sizable teams of underwriters. Insurers are starting to use AI and other technologies to speed their underwriting decisions from their current one to five days down to seconds and to reduce manual underwriting operations altogether. AI will increasingly play a large role in improving the quality of TC Insurer's credit decisions and is intended to result in lower credit losses, greater operational efficiencies, and overall improved client services.

TCI CONTRACT MANAGEMENT AND ADMINISTRATION APPLICATIONS

TCI Contract management systems are used to enable an insured and any partners relying on its TCI (e.g., Financiers) to confirm when each of its AR are in fact meeting the conditions for coverage under their TCI Contract and to adhere to deadlines for filing claims or sending required notices to the TC Insurer to maintain coverage. Without these systems, insureds must manually refer to their TCI Contracts periodically to ensure their AR are compliant with their Contract conditions. More advanced TCI Contract management tools may provide the insured and any third parties it authorizes with valuable credit data about each of its Buyers' payment behavior. For example, these systems can reveal when Buyers pay their Invoices, the level of any Dilution, and relevant trends in payment behaviors, all of which are valuable for evaluating AR creditworthiness and for purposes of determining appropriate Credit Terms and pricing.

CHAPTER 8

Careers in TF

The TF industry is vast and global, offering exceptionally rewarding and exciting career opportunities with ample room for creativity, innovation, teamwork, and professional growth. It also provides great opportunities for global and domestic travel, and to engage and transact with diverse groups of clients and counterparts around the world. The range of TF employers and job types for professionals at all levels is extensive and continually growing. Many TF jobs involve working for banks, finance companies, TC Insurers and Brokers, FinTechs, national governments, and international finance Agencies. Many other types of companies involved in TF also hire professionals to negotiate, execute, and manage their TF needs. Sellers and Buyers, for example, hire specialists to manage their AR, Trade Payables, and other TF activities. Similarly, service providers that facilitate TF transactions, such as attorneys, accountants, shippers, freight forwarders, and business software and FinTech developers, employ people with special TF skills or expertise.

The key job qualifications to be a successful TF professional include the ability to listen and understand a client's or transaction party's specific objectives, and the ability to identify, access, and apply the most appropriate TF tools and techniques to address those objectives. It also helps to have strong interpersonal, verbal, and written communication skills to be able to interact effectively with diverse groups of clients and other transaction participants from different parts of the world. TF arrangers and structurers often need to be able to explain transaction details, risks, and rewards to multiple parties, including the appropriate internal and external parties from whom approvals and support may be necessary. Foreign language expertise may be helpful for regionally focused specialists, but is by no means a general employment requirement. Similarly, formal business, financial, or accounting training, while potentially helpful, is not a general requirement for a successful TF professional. As a rule, the most effective TF professionals will be those with the ability to understand and apply the widest range of TF tools appropriately and who possess the imagination and creativity to find solutions to achieve TF's fundamental objectives for the parties.

TF EMPLOYERS

Below is a summary of the typical TF employers and the types of positions they might offer.

Financiers

Financiers globally are large employers of TF professionals. A Financier's TF teams may be called Trade Services, International Trade, Global Trade Finance, Transaction Banking, Treasury Services, Working Capital Solutions, or various other names. A Large Financier will often organize its TF offerings under a single TF group composed of distinct specialty teams. For example, a large global Financier is likely to have a global TF group, under which there are distinct teams for AR Purchase Finance, SCF, Agency Finance, and probably a Letter of Credit or Trade Services team. Some of these teams may be combined into a single group. Other organizations may have a more siloed approach or may combine some TF teams with other less related groups within a Financier (e.g., investment banking, leasing, asset-based lending, cash management, treasury solutions). No matter how a TF offering is organized, specialists will be dedicated to each TF product offering, with some members of the TF team addressing more than one TF solution. Medium and small Financiers may have smaller teams that handle only one or more products.

Government and Internal Agencies

Agencies are a good source of entry level and senior TF jobs. They typically provide a wide range of TF products in a variety of capacities, including being a Financier, Guarantor, and TC Insurer. They also have a relatively large internal organization featuring in-house legal teams, credit and loan officers, claims and recovery specialists, marketing and sales professionals, and transactors. The following is a small sample of government and international agencies providing TF jobs:

- Export Credit Agencies (ECAs)
- World Bank
- International Finance Agency (IFC)
- Multilateral Insurance and Guarantee Agency (MIGA)
- European Bank for Reconstruction and Development (EBRD)
- Asian Development Bank (ADB)
- Banco Latinoamericano de Comercio Exterior (BLADEX)
- The Inter-American Development Bank (IADB)
- Trade Promotion Offices, Exporter Assistance Offices
- US International Development Finance Corporation (DFC)
- US Small Business Administration (SBA)

- US International Trade Administration (ITA)
- US State Export Assistance and Business Development Offices

Types of TF Positions

Depending on the size of a business or Agency, the following positions and functions are typically handled by one or more teams or people:

- New Business Origination, Sales, Marketing.
- Structuring and arranging transactions.
- Product Specialists.
- Product Management: Manage scope of existing and new TF products and permitted product variations.
- Transaction Implementation, Contract Execution, Administration, and Monitoring.
- Client service representatives.
- Credit and Loan Officers that assess and approve credit and transaction risks.
- Compliance: KYC, Anti-money laundering officer.
- Trade Debt Distribution and syndication.
- TCI specialists and underwriters.
- Innovation teams that assess, innovate, and implement new technologies and processes.
- Product or Group team managers covering one or more products, regionally or globally.

Trade Credit Insurance Providers: TCI Insurers, Brokers, and Agents

- Risk Underwriter: assesses and approves Buyer and Obligor Credit Risks.
- Commercial Underwriter: negotiates and structures TCI Contracts.
- Credit Information and risk rating teams that gather financial information and produce Buyer and Obligor risk ratings.
- Business Operations (aka back office): Contract implementation, monitoring, administration, customer service, billing.
- Sales for new business origination and existing business retention: liaison for client and Broker contacts, delivering quotes and negotiating terms.
- Claims team that assesses, adjusts, and approves claims.
- Legal team that manages general corporate and regulatory matters as well as specific TCI Contract matters, including negotiating and documenting contract terms.

- Compliance officers that manage and enforce KYC in conformity with the various laws, regulations, and internal compliance policies.
- Finance and Treasury, providing accounting, financial reporting, tax management, payroll, claim payments, and all other financial matters.

Corporate Sellers and Buyers

- Customer Finance, Treasury, Procurement and Payables, Credit Managers, Client Solutions.

Logistics Providers

- Transportation, Shipping, customs, licensing, certifications, inspections.

Law Offices

- Attorneys and Paralegals: negotiating and documenting TF transactions; providing legal advice and opinions regarding transaction enforceability and legal risks; addressing disputes among transaction parties.